twin stories

twin stories

Their Mysterious and Unique Bond

Susan Kohl

Wildcat Canyon Press
A Division of Circulus Publishing Group, Inc.
Berkeley, California

Twin Stories: Their Mysterious and Unique Bond

Publisher: Tamara Traeder
Marketing Director: Carol Brown
Editorial Director: Roy M. Carlisle
Managing Editor: Leyza Yardley
Production Coordinator: Larissa Berry
Copyeditor: Jean Blomquist
Proofreader: Leia Carlton
Cover Design: Mary Beth Salmon
Interior Design and Typesetting: A Page Turner

Typographic Specifications: Text in Walbaum 10.5/16, headings in Insignia.

Printed in Canada

Cataloging-in-Publication Data
Kohl, Susan, 1959-
     Twin stories: their mysterious and unique bond / by Susan Kohl.
         p. cm.
     ISBN 1-885171-58-7
     1. Twins. 2. Twins—Psychology. I. Title.
BF723.T9 K64 2001
155.44'4—dc21

                                                                              2001035513

Distributed to the trade by Publishers Group West
10 9 8 7 6 5 4 3 2 1   01 02 03 04 05

This book is dedicated to the special twins in my life—

My sons, Sam and Max Kohl

And to the memory of Bob Lawrence, who passed on
during the writing of this book.

The Blessings of We

Miracles happen, one happened to me,

when a blessing of one, became

the blessings of we.

A bond before birth, a bond

beyond time, two souls

created in sharing, your story

is mine.

When one of us leaves, two

continue to be, a mirror's

reflection – you, me, and we.

By Douglas F. Kohl

Contents

Acknowledgments

As you read this book, you will find that the stories woven throughout have been told with great honesty. On that note, I must also be honest and admit that I could not have completed this book without the love and support of a large number of people. I would like to thank my husband, Doug, for taking care of our boys, the house, and the business while I was chained to my computer. I would also like to thank my eldest son, Frank, for helping out in all the special ways he does. My twins, Sam and Max, were, of course, the inspiration for this book, and I want to thank them for bringing such joy into our lives. I would also like to recognize Frank and Frances; Lela, who lost her twin, Lola, one day after birth; Adrienne and Mark; Larry and Lana; and Penny and Skip, all who make up my family network of twins. Finally, I would like to thank my parents, Bill and Rosemary Cloughley, for always helping whenever they can, regardless of whether I'm writing a book.

On a professional note, I would like to acknowledge Roy M. Carlisle and Tamara Traeder of Wildcat Canyon Press for giving me this wonderful opportunity. They are, without question, the best in the business and terrific to work with. I would like to thank Carol Brown, Patsy Barich, Leyza Yardley, Larissa Berry, Nenelle

Bunnin, and the entire staff of Wildcat Canyon Press for their professionalism and expertise in making this book the best it can be. I would also like to recognize Jean M. Blomquist for a great job in copyediting, and Mary Beth Salmon, a mother of twins, for the delightful cover design.

I would like to thank the organizers of Twins Days. Their festival opened my eyes to the world of twins and for that I am deeply grateful. I am also grateful to the twins who let me interrupt their pancake breakfast or barge into personal conversations at the festival in order to get some terrific interviews. The twins at Twins Days were so open, honest, and friendly that I'm sure they will be an inspiration to all who read this book. I would also like to thank the twins who came to me through other family and friends as well as through the public relations community.

Last, I would like to thank Dr. Raymond Brandt for making it possible to interview his beloved twinless twins. I cannot say enough about him, also a twinless twin, and these courageous people who went out on a limb publicly in order to share their stories of loss and deep grief. Thank you so much.

This book has been a true labor of love for me because of the subject and because of all the people who helped me achieve this wonderful feeling of accomplishment. Thank you all.

A Word from the Author

Mother of Twins

It's not hard for me to remember when my fascination with twins first began. I had been the typical career woman, working as a television news journalist in Orlando, Florida, and enjoying the freedom and travel that came when there were only husband and wife. After about three years of fun and few responsibilities, my husband, Doug, and I developed a new set of priorities and decided that we would start our family.

I soon got pregnant and we rejoiced. We also speculated. My father-in-law was a fraternal twin, so everyone on my husband's side joked that perhaps Doug and I would have twins. I didn't have twins anywhere on my side of the family, and I had never known a set of twins personally. The fact was that neither of us knew much about them so we mistakenly believed all the old wives' tales about twins skipping generations. Needless to say we believed we had a very good chance to become the next in the Kohl family to have a multiple birth.

Well, August 31, 1991 came—and so did Frank William Kohl, our first son. There was only one of him, so Doug and I went on with our lives, enjoying first-time parenthood and never giving another thought to having twins. I became pregnant again in 1993, and imagine my surprise when, at seven weeks, my ultrasound technician said, "I see one baby—I see two babies!" I was totally unprepared, but elated. As my mother-in-law likes to say, I was about to do what no one in the Kohl family had done for the past seventy years—produce a set of twins.

Sam Forrest and Max Douglas Kohl arrived on March 11, 1994. The doctors said they were identical, and from the trouble we had telling them apart, we thought so too. (We later learned that identical twins have nothing to do with heredity; it is just a stroke of luck when an egg splits and you are blessed with two babies instead of one.) We read everything we could find on twins. There was plenty of information on the care and feeding of twins, but nothing on the special bond that these two little people would develop from day one.

As they grew, I became fascinated by their behavior: the way they played together, the things they were willing to put up with, the selflessness they seemed to show when making decisions that involved them both. I began to wonder what kind of lives they would lead as they grew older, and if their special bond would blossom or fade away. I also wondered if there was a road map of sorts that would give me a "heads-up" about what to expect during their childhood and beyond. Finally, I wanted to learn from twins themselves what I could do to help my boys become healthy, happy, and well-adjusted human beings.

I began to think about writing a book about twins. When you have a set of twins, people come out of the woodwork to tell you that they are a twin, or have a set of twins in the family, or know a set. There is an abundance of twins in the world today, thanks to smarter doctors, better prenatal care, and, of course, fertility drugs. My initial thoughts about writing a book were validated time and time again.

When I finally decided to pursue the book and told people about my idea, I was told in no uncertain terms to "Go to Twinsburg." Twinsburg is a small town in Ohio that holds an annual three-day festival, called Twins Days. I went to the festival in August of 2000, and what I experienced there was a wondrous thing. There were nearly three thousand sets of twins in attendance—most of them dressed exactly alike—and oh, did they have stories. As they shared very personal life experiences with me, I began to get a glimpse of what life would be like for my boys, now age six. I listened to tales about growing up as a twin, the benefits, the fun, and the frustrations. I recognized some of the behaviors of my own twins and could empathize with the feelings of the twins I interviewed because I had witnessed those feelings firsthand. I saw many similarities between twin sets, and a few surprising differences. And I began to realize just what an incredible gift my twins have been given.

Today when my twins are fighting or unhappy with one another, I want to make them understand just how lucky they are and convince them that they need to cherish each other. I want to convey the things I saw in Twinsburg—the connection, the unspoken communication, and the unconditional love. I realize that they are just six years old now, but the time will soon come when they are old enough to understand.

I wanted to write this book to give readers, including my sons, personal insight into the range of emotions and experiences twins—mainly identicals and same-sex fraternals—have throughout their lives. I have interviewed twin sets ranging in ages from six to eighty-six, from all walks of life. I have interviewed men and women who have lost a twin and have never felt the same since.

After spending hours on the phone, corresponding via e-mail, and interviewing twins in person, I have come to two very important conclusions. Most sets celebrate their twinness; all abhor being treated like freaks.

Whether you are a twin, or have twins in your family or in your circle of friends, it is my hope that this book will give you a greater understanding of the special relationship two people can have when they have shared the same womb at the same time. Theirs is a strong and powerful bond that neither time nor distance seems to shake. If you are a twin, I hope you will not only celebrate your twinness but also cherish it, for it is truly remarkable. If you are a parent, teacher, family member, or friend, I hope you will learn from these stories and gain a greater respect for these unique relationships. Above all, I hope you enjoy reading these twin stories as much as I have enjoyed writing about them.

CHAPTER ONE

What We Know

"People don't get it. Our husbands don't get it. Our children don't get it. But they love it. To them, being a twin is something uncanny." Those are the words of forty-two-year-old Linda Houk and her identical twin sister, Laura Fryman. They echo the thoughts of people around the world when it comes to the subject of twins. Twins are unusual, sometimes a little intimidating, but above all, fascinating.

What do we know about twins? We know that twins are very common, fun to know and study, and usually have something that most of us don't have—an amazing bond with a sibling born on the same day. Most enjoy the special attention they receive, yet are frustrated by it at times. Being a twin has its ups and downs, but as you will read, for most being a twin is a blessing to celebrate.

Turning Heads

According to twin researcher Nancy L. Segal, Ph.D., there are approximately 73 million twin pairs, or 146 million individual twins, in the world today.[1] Ask anyone you know and chances are they either have a set of twins in the family or personally know a twin.

Our fascination with twins is neither new nor surprising. Peter Whitmer, Ph.D., wrote these words about twins in his book *The Inner Elvis,* which explored the life of Elvis Presley, who lost his twin brother at birth: "In man's collective consciousness, twins are a living metaphor. They represent the richness of life, the sources of life, the perpetuation of life; they are life, itself, standing in exaggerated form. At the same time, there is a shadowy and unknown dimension to twins. There is an enduring allure to the mystery of twins."[2]

It's impossible to try to attach a date to the beginning of our insatiable interest in twinning. But it's important to note that our fascination with twins was not always a positive one. In 1884, George H. Napheys, A.M., M.D., wrote a book entitled *The Physical Life of Woman: Advice to the Maiden, Wife and Mother.*[3] He had some rather alarming ideas about the mystery of twins: "As a rule, a woman has one child at a time. Twins, when they occur, are looked upon with disfavor by most people. There is a popular notion that twins are apt to be wanting in physical and mental vigor. Among the relatives of imbeciles and idiots, twin bearing is common. Monsters born without brains have rarely occurred except among twins."

At the time of his writing, Dr. Napheys estimated that the birth of twins occurred once in about eighty deliveries. That estimate holds true in North America today. But clearly he was mistaken in his observation of twinning as a freak occurrence and an aberration of nature.

Today everywhere we turn twins are celebrated. Not a day goes by that we don't see articles in the newspapers or stories on the radio and television about twins. Our interest runs the gamut from celebrities and politicians, to athletes and entertainers. In the summer of 2000, the world was fascinated by twin athletes Paul and Morgan Hamm, who served on the U.S. Olympic gymnastic team in Sydney, and the identical twin runners, Alvin and Calvin Harrison, who ran the first and third legs of the men's 4x400 meter relay to help win the Olympic gold for the United States.

On the political front, during his bid for the presidency, candidate George W. Bush carefully tried to protect the privacy of his eighteen-year-old fraternal twin daughters, Barbara and Jenna, under intense national exposure. They would head off to college in the fall of 2000, yet despite his efforts, they often made the "A" section of newspapers across the country.[4] And then there was the nationwide coverage of Ron and Don Mosbaugh, fifty-six-year-old identical twin brothers who ran against each other for the Jasper County, Missouri, coroner's spot in the November 2000 local election. Ron was the Republican and Don, the Democrat. They appeared several times on ABC's *Good Morning America*—for the fun of it. Incumbent Ron won the election, by the way. His brother somehow didn't seem to mind too much.

On the celebrity front, America has been fascinated with many twins. In 1950, Jeanne and Eleanor Fulstone, identical twins from Smith Valley, Nevada, won a nationwide contest to become the "All-American Toni Twins." The Toni Home Permanent Company wanted a pair of wholesome young beauties to participate in an advertising campaign promoting their new home permanent product. In those days, the only choice for curly hair was a twenty dollar cold wave. The premise of the ad was "Which Twin has the Toni?" Eleanor happened to be the lucky one and gave herself the Toni while Jeanne had the more expensive, lengthy permanent wave process. The twins traveled across the country and Europe where they were toasted everywhere they went. It was a glorious time for the twins, and the world loved them.

In 1959, Joan Boyd and Jayne Schwartz, twenty-one-year-old identical twins, became household names as the original Doublemint twins, seen in commercials up to twenty times a day. Twins continue to be featured in Doublemint advertisements to this day.

In 1987, Mary-Kate and Ashley Olsen, fraternal twins that look identical, shared the role of Michelle on a television sitcom called *Full House*. When the show ended in 1995, America was so enthralled with the pair that it supported just about every project the twins did. Today they are touted as among the most highly paid child celebrities in the country and certainly one of the hottest acts in children's entertainment. They have infiltrated just about every sector of the entertainment business—television, video, film, dolls, complementary print publications, the Web, and even clothing. They are rumored to be worth more than $100 million.[5]

Several male-twin pairs have relished in the entertainment spotlight as well. Currently two of the most popular surfers on the Association of Surfing Professionals (ASP) World Tour are twins—C. J. and Damien Hobgood. They're smart, blonde, extremely talented, and no strangers to the attention of young women around the globe. In December 2000, another pair of male teenage heartthrobs took center stage.

The singing duo Evan and Jaron Lowenstein hit *Billboard* magazine's music charts with an explosive single called "Crazy for This Girl." The nineteen-year-old musicians perfectly complemented each other and were fascinating to watch and hear.

Another dynamic duo in the spotlight was the famous Barbi twins. Hugh Hefner wasted no time signing the double beauties to appear for the celebrity cover of *Playboy* magazine.[6] His intuition about the world's awe of twins proved correct when that issue sold out in just two weeks. *Playboy* signed the twins to do a second layout, which became the largest-selling issue in *Playboy* history. They recently came out with a book called *Barbi Twins: Dying to Be Healthy.* While the book focuses on millennium dieting and nutrition, it also chronicles the twins' shared journey to recovery after living through food addictions and eating disorders.

The list of famous twins goes on and on. In 1996, NASA jumped onto the twin bandwagon by naming identical brothers to its astronaut corps. Both were selected to become space shuttle pilots. In 2000, there was the live birth of the Bognar twins on the Internet. And then there was America's fascination with *Survivor's* single-mother castaway, Jenna Lewis, who left her twin girls behind to try to win a million dollars by being the last "voted off the island."

There is no question about the widespread fascination with twins. When I first mentioned my idea for this book to people, the response was overwhelming. A well-respected reporter for the *Wall Street Journal* sent me an e-mail that said, "Everyone loves a good twin story." I believe the reporter is right.

How Does It Happen

There are few rational answers to the mysteries surrounding the subject of twins despite many attempts by myths and old wives' tales to explain the unexplainable. It seems that very few of us understand how these enigmatic people come to be. As Dr. Nancy Segal says in her book, *Entwined Lives,* "What produces twins, who has twins and how twins differ from singletons, or nontwins, are among the vital questions that have fueled debates over the role of twins in scientific investigation."[7]

We know that identical twins result when a single fertilized egg divides between the first and fourteenth day after conception. According to E. M. Bryan, author of *The Nature and Nurture of Twins,* there is little evidence that the tendency to produce identical twins is tied to genes.[8] Many researchers believe that identical twinning happens randomly. The old wives' tales about skipping generations on the father's side is simply not true when it comes to identicals. Having identical twins today is considered just the luck of the draw. Although, the scientific community agrees there should be more research into how and why identicals occur. There is truth to the genetic notion, however, that women can pass along the ability to produce more than one egg, which results in fraternal twins. Fraternal twins occur when the mother produces two eggs at the same time and both are fertilized.

Now comes the mind-boggling question. Why do some identicals look different while some fraternals look very similar? A DNA test is the only way to tell with a high degree of certainty whether twins are identical. In the case of my sons Sam and Max, the pediatricians predicted that they were identical based upon examination of the placenta immediately after birth. The fact that no one could tell them apart somewhat confirmed that theory. Fortunately for us, they were not identical in every way. Max has a birthmark on his neck, and Max is, and has always been, slightly heavier than Sam. Researchers say that differences in the quantity of nutrition reaching each twin might explain the size difference, but there is also a chance that the doctors could have been wrong. We are not 100 percent sure they are identical and that uncertainty is frustrating. They look so much alike, yet twin experts say fraternal twins can also look quite similar because they have the ability to inherit the same genes from each parent.

The Bond

Regardless of whether a twin is identical or same-sex fraternal, there are few I have found that do not share a very special bond. This bond manifests itself in trust, compatibility, attachment, and loyalty. It is evident whether spoken or unspoken and some say it is stronger than the bond between mother and child, or husband and wife.

Jennifer and Penelope Waggoner, age twenty-seven, agree. "This is just special, like soul to soul," said Penelope. "It's a much deeper emotional bond, and that bond is always there. I have tried to explain it to my boyfriend. He is curious, but he doesn't really know how close we are. If we spoke with another set of twins, I'm sure they would understand the connection."

Donna DeLozier and Dianne Guthrie are sixty-one-year-old identical twins living in different states. They try to get together every six or eight weeks and while the short, infrequent visits aren't enough to satisfy their need for each other, they feel that their bond endures. "It's like always having a best friend," said Donna. "She is someone I can depend on, someone who is always there for me."

"If you were a twin, you'd see this is a different world," said Chris Scamahorne who lives with his nineteen-year-old twin brother, Jon. "We do everything together," said Jon. "We are like best friends. We hang out together. We like the same kind of clothes—the same styles. We don't dress alike on a daily basis, but every once in a while we do like to wear the same clothes to go to clubs or hang out with friends. We have a unique relationship that has its ups and downs."

For seventeen year-old Caramie and Crystal Green, being identical twins has proven to be an emotional lifesaver on at least one occasion. Caramie recalled a very traumatic time. "I came home from work one Sunday morning in January and found Crystal very upset. I asked her what was wrong and she could not tell me. Seeing my other half cry so much tore me apart. She finally sobbed that one of our closest friends had passed away after being drugged with GHB. Crystal was too upset to attend the ceremony, so I went alone. I presented our friend's casket with two baby pink roses—one from me and the other was from my twin. When I returned home, I told Crystal what I had done, she hugged me. From then on, we have become so unbelievably close. I am so blessed to have a twin sister and I know she feels the same way."

Just Another Sibling?

As I mentioned previously, my father-in-law, Frank J. Kohl, is a fraternal twin. His sister, Frances Handlong, lives in Missouri. They have been separated for most of their adult lives. My sister-in-law, Adrienne Lille Kohl, is also a fraternal twin. Her brother, Mark, lives not too far from her in the San Francisco Bay Area. I have talked to both of my in-laws extensivley about being twins, and for them, the "twin experience" is not as strong.

Frank and Frances and Adrienne and Mark all grew up in large families. Early on they were paired with older siblings who were responsible for watching them and making sure they stayed out of trouble. While each twin is fond of the other, today they could almost be categorized as just another sibling. After listening to the stories and talking to relatives, however, it's apparent that there was a twin connection in their youth. Adrienne's mother, Rita Lille, reminisces that when Adrienne and Mark were babies, they seemed to be very attached to one another.

"They were very close as toddlers," said Rita, "Adrienne was three minutes older than Mark. I don't know if it was the female thing or a dominant twin thing or what but she would take over the lead. One story we still laugh about today is a common occurrence that happened when they would be in the playpen together. Adrienne would stand up and get her hands in Mark's hair. He would holler, then I would take her out and he would holler louder because she was gone.

"They each walked practically on the same day at twelve months. She was larger, but he would eat more and say, 'I'll eat Adrienne's.' In the beginning, she was the leader. She would give him orders. He was the follower. Eventually, it was different.

"Twins were not uncommon in my family," Rita continued. "My sister had fraternal twins. My cousin had fraternal twins. I had made it a point with Adrienne and Mark to rarely refer to them as twins, always the babies, always Adrienne and Mark. They are very much individuals today."

The same is true for Frank and Frances Kohl. They started out very close as small children but grew into two very independent people leading two very successful lives. "We were pretty close when we were small until about the age of ten or twelve.

"Because of the way our family worked, I didn't even know I was a twin," Frank added. "Catherine, my older sister, was assigned to take care of me. Another sister, Muriel, was assigned to take care of Frances."

"Frank didn't realize how popular he was in high school and I was always so proud of him," said Frances. "Even to this day, I am proud that he's my twin because of his achievements in life."

"We stay in touch still but not as much as when we were younger. This is partly due to the fact that we were busy raising our families and that we live far apart," said Frances. Frances has lived in Missouri nearly her entire life and Frank moved to California when he was a young man.

Frank, twin to Frances, and Adrienne, twin to Mark, became products of their environments. Because they were different sexes, they naturally went their own ways in school and sports, with friends, and later in life. They also had other brothers and sisters to play with and depend on. They were not brought up to focus on their twinness and were encouraged to become individuals, so they have.

However, I believe there are some boy-girl twins who are very connected. One pair stands out in my mind. Shortly after my twins, Sam and Max, were born, a family moved in next door to us. We rejoiced. They had toddler twins! I was looking forward to visiting with the mother and absorbing all of her secrets to raising twins. Her twins were adorable boy-girl fraternals who wore boy-girl clothes in the same fabric. They had no other siblings and were very close. As they grew older, we watched them cling to one another and go through a difficult time interacting socially with other children. Again I believe they were products of their environment. Their family unit was very tight and rarely visited with other families. The children did not go to preschool or out for "play dates." In this case, the twins only had each other.

I don't think it's fair to stereotype twins, whether they are identical, same-sexed fraternals, or boy-girl twins, but I think you can say that family situations play a key role in any child's development. When boy-girl twins have other siblings, they tend to be less close than those who have only each other. Yet identical twins, and often same-sexed fraternals, tend to be close no matter what the family circumstances. But then there are the twins, who, no matter what the circumstances, are not close at all—perhaps because their twinness was forced upon them to such an extent that they rebel. The one common denominator, found in almost all of the twins I've met and interviewed, is that they take great pride in being twins and that they have unconditional love for their twin, no matter what.

The Twin Roller-Coaster

There are few twins who will claim that their lives are picture perfect. The ups and downs vary depending on the twins themselves. There are the twins who live together, celebrating their twinness every minute of the day. There are twins who are apart but live in close proximity. And there are a few that have put time and distance between them to escape from their twinness.

Thirty-four-year-old Rhonda Kulpinski and Renee Richardson are identical twins who, for the longest time, did not enjoy the twin experience. In a letter to the Twinsburg, Ohio, Twins Days Festival committee, Renee wrote, "As with many twins, we grew up being dressed alike and perceived as the same person (our cousins even blended our names—Ronanee—because they did not know which twin was which).[9]

"Rhonda and I fought our twinness by rebelling against each other as we hit our early teens, separating to the point in which we had no relationship, not even as sisters. It is normally around seventeen to eighteen years of age that twins begin to come together again, but at the age of sixteen our twin path divided and did not come together for fourteen years. We were close neither in geography nor emotion.

"Then in a rare phone conversation, my sister mentioned that she had heard about some kind of twin festival. We attended the annual Twins Days Festival in Twinsburg, Ohio, with our mother. It was nice but weird for us to meet so many twins who could not fathom living apart. We felt like oddballs because we were so independent of each other. We could not relate to their closeness. Still, a seed was planted. Now I can't imagine being separated from her love again."

Le Melcher, a forty-one-year-old identical twin, reflects on what it must be like to ignore the special bond that most twins have. "I know that some twins are unhappy that they are twins. I don't feel that way at all. I do admit there were times in high school when I was mad at Pete. He would have offended somebody and I would be the one in trouble. I would wonder why this guy was slugging me in the hallway when I was just walking by. Well, my brother forgot to warn me that he was in a row with this person. Still, we both enjoyed the comfort of knowing the other was there, and we could never have a fight so big that we would never talk again."

"You've got a friend for life," explained Andrew Hill, age thirty-five. "For the twins that don't get along, I just don't understand what their problem is. They're missing something extremely sacred and special."

"Regret is the most expensive word in the dictionary," said Andrew's twin, Anthony. You see all of these twins going on television and talking about their petty disagreements. You lose so much time that way. I think as years go by they will really regret not getting to know their twin, and not enjoying the bond they should and could have."

A Special Relationship

Even at a young age, most twins recognize their special relationship. At age six, Sam or Max will often surprise my husband and I by selflessly giving up a toy or a treat in order for his brother to have something. Their disagreements are minor and often fleeting. They miss each other when one is gone, yet they are happy for the brother who gets to do something on his own.

Ten-year-old twins Alysha and Alexandria Chmielewski Schall can relate. "In college we want to be roommates, and we want to live next door to each other when we grow up. We say to each other—I don't want to ever leave you. I've been with you all of my life."

"We don't know what it's like not to be a twin," said Joan Pahls Notch, sister to forty-year-old identical twin Jeannie Van Horn. "We have always had each other. We have always been each other's best friend. There is definitely an advantage to being a twin."

Good Twin, Bad Twin

Throughout history, twins have always received extra attention—from family members, from friends, and from perfect strangers. With this recognition and fascination also comes some baggage.

Patricia Malmstrom, in an article entitled "Good Twin, Bad Twin," writes that twins are up against the human penchant for comparing, contrasting, and labeling.[10] She says since twins are born a "matched set," so to speak, they are often appropriated as symbols of the good and bad in all of us. She cites a well-known example in the Old Testament: the story of the twins Jacob and Esau. Their mother, Rebecca, fueled a rivalry between them with far-reaching consequences because she favored the sensitive and cultivated Jacob over his more impulsive twin, Esau.

For Daphne Koenigsberg and Dawn Jordan, age forty, the story hits close to home. Daphne shared, "The good twin, bad twin label was put on us on the day we came home from the hospital, actually the day we were born. Dawn was more independent and she started showing that very early. She knew more of what she wanted and because of that, she always fought for what she wanted. So she was labeled the bad twin from the very beginning.

"One of the things we have always known is how close we actually are," continued Daphne. "And we have overcome all of the baggage. We now understand why it happened and where it came from. Nothing is perfect in your life anyway, and it's just something that we had to learn how to deal with. I've always had the burden of being the 'good twin' even though I was just like the rest. The truth is I wasn't that good."

Frustrations

As a twin, you have a lot to deal with. There are twin myths, twin stereotypes, and twin expectations. There are also plenty of twin frustrations that can occur on a daily basis. Fortunately the frustrations are fairly common, and twins quickly learn to handle them.

Stephanie Winger and Jennifer Wilcox, thirty-one, are also fraternal twins. They say they don't look alike but are the same height and have the same color hair. Some people think they're identical and others can't even tell they are sisters. Stephanie commented, "The best thing about being a twin is that you have someone your own age with whom you can go through life's little experiences simultaneously. Growing up, the thing I most didn't care for were the people who think of you as one person instead of two individuals. People called us 'the twins or twinees.'"

"People ask, 'Are you Linda or are you Laura?'" said Laura Fryman. "I hate that. And then I have always been called 'Linda's sister.'"

Jon Scamahorne commiserates: "It's not bad, but sometimes it is when people ask, 'Which one are you?' It's a little bit frustrating."

Maria and Angela DeCaprio say they can't blame people too much for getting their identities confused. They are sixteen years old and seem to have an understanding of why people act the way they do. "We are different than most of the people in the world. It's a good thing, but sometimes it can be bad. People give you the same presents or call you by the other one's name. It is annoying especially when your parents call you by the wrong name. Sometimes our parents can't tell us apart."

"I know a lot of people who see us for the first time are definitely confused," said Dean Jenson, twenty-three-year-old identical twin to David. "They think we look alike, but people who know us can't figure out how someone could get us confused. My brother wears khakis and polos; for me it's jeans and a T-shirt or shorts and a T-shirt. You'd think people would at least figure that out. We definitely have our own style of dressing.

"At times, you get frustrated with people not being able to tell who is who. I set people up with computers. People are always coming up to my brother with their computer problems. I know he hates it. One time I was sitting in an accounting class that David had taken a year or two before. The professor called me David. The same thing happened with the dean of the college. He mixed us up once, and then made it a point to call each of us by the wrong names just to be funny. It's not really funny."

Jenna and Jessi Clayton are fourteen, and they have the same kind of problems. "Everywhere we go people ask if we are sisters and we tell them we are twins," said Jenna. "Sometimes they will ask if we are twins. They act like it is the weirdest thing in the world. What's really frustrating is when the yearbook committee at school gets our pictures wrong."

The dashing Hill twins, thirty-five, echoed those thoughts. "I've always believed that being twins, everybody wants to think of you as one person," said Andrew.

Anthony agreed, "It's really hard to set yourselves apart when you're children because you've got outside influences that dictate whether you're one person or two."

Le Melcher, forty-one, agrees: "Sadly, there are a lot of people who, if they can't tell you apart, think you're the same person. That is good and bad. On the positive side, my twin's successes work to my benefit and open doors. Sometimes people aren't quite sure which twin I am so they welcome me with open arms. Now if my twin, Pete, were a mass murderer and they were confused about my identity, they would shut the door in a heartbeat," he laughs.

Jeannie Van Horn, forty, also finds a bit of humor in the twin frustration situation: "I think it is funny when people ask your age and when you were born and then sure enough turn around and ask your twin the same thing. That falls into the freaky things that people say without thinking."

When asked if there is anything bad about being a twin, twins rarely give you answers of substance. Most agree that it's pretty neat being two instead of one. Once in a while you might hear a complaint or two, but they always seem very mild. Such is the case with forty-two-year-old Beth Whitaker and Judy Fischer. Beth said, "Judy knows which buttons to push. All siblings fight, but twins know how to push

22

those buttons a little more. They know what makes you tick because they are so intimate with you. But I must say, we've had a great time being twins!"

Chris and Jon Scamahorne, age nineteen, say their only complaint is the competition in other people's minds. As Chris puts it, "Everyone tries to compare us and everyone has his or her own opinions. They instantly form impressions about us." Jon added, "Wherever twins go, you are always being compared to each other. It gets annoying after a while. Just because you're in a bad mood one day doesn't mean you are always like that. Chris is the outspoken one and I'm more laid back. People seem to really tune into that and stereotype us."

The Joys

When you ask twins what they think is the very best thing about being a twin, the answers do not vary much at all. Twins have someone to share in their journey through life. Together they can overcome obstacles and eliminate discouragement. They gain emotional power and renew inner strength through each other. Someone is always there to help mend their broken spirits. They are all the best parts of each other's soul.

"We've never had a point in our lives where we wish we hadn't been twins. It has always been the two of us," said Beth Whitacker and Judy Fischer.

"The connection is something that nothing in the world could ever replace or even match," said Owen Murphy, twenty-four, of his fraternal brother, Adam. "Despite all of the shortcomings we may experience in life, it's all worth it to be a twin."

"A twin is much closer than a best friend or a beloved spouse," said Retha Fielding, age fifty, of her identical sister, Letha Bell. "This other person is part of my heart."

Tara Behnke, thirty, is a fraternal same-sex twin who is just as close as any identical twin would be. "We are even closer than any best friends you could ever have. We know just about everything there is to know about each other. We spend just about every minute together. We go out on the weekends together, we work together, we come home pick up the phone and call each other. We are very close."

"It is not the amount of physical time twins spend together that creates this twin bond," said Linda N. Rutherford, who, today, is a twinless twin. "The bond begins at birth and continues during the course of a lifetime."

Michelle Turner, a twinless twin, believes this too. "I think the relationship my sister and I had is the closest you can ever have. It's the same feeling you have for a child, except that it's more of a selfish feeling because it's part of you. With a child, you can love him or her with all of your heart and you want to take care of that person. With my twin and me, we were part of each other."

"I believe the best part of being a twin is that you never really feel alone—even when you are apart," said Tom Carlock, of his now deceased identical twin, Tim. "The twin bond is tremendously strong and extremely hard to explain on a scientific level. I would like to tell other twins just how precious this bond is. I tell twins all the time not to take anything for granted and to experience as much as you can together. I believe the bond will always go on."

The undeniable fascination we all have about the bond between twins, fraternal or identical, is just as intriguing to twins themselves. And the more we all learn about this bond the more mysterious it seems.

CHAPTER TWO

Growing Up in Tandem

Admit it. We're only human so it's hard not to sneak a peek at twins or even to stare at them when they're not looking. After all, identical twins are one of the marvels and mysteries of life: two human beings—the product of one egg, and identical clones of one another. Most twins have an intense connection to each other that we singletons are intrigued by.

An Outsider's Curiosity

I myself am guilty of watching my twins, Sam and Max, intently whenever I can. My eyes often switch from the face of one to the other as I look for similarities and differences. Because they have not yet had DNA testing, there is always that morsel of doubt if they are truly identical. So I take inventory. Yes, I calculate. I think to myself, that's the same nose, their lips are the same, but why does Sam have a freckle and Max does not? I do the same thing when I spy twins from afar or when I get the chance to inspect them up close. I study photographs of twins in books and magazines and again I take inventory.

Twins get my attention—without fail. And I am not alone. I know it and twins in general know it too.

At seventy years of age, Betty Burton and Bert Polley can vouch for a lifetime of looks, stares, and gawks. "We get a lot of attention. We went on a Hawaiian cruise and you would have thought we were movie stars the way everyone stared at us."

Dennis and Kenneth Jacob know the feeling. "At first I didn't really like it that much," said Kenneth. "When we were in middle school, we were both on the shy side and did not like the attention. As we got older, we matured and now the attention is kind of fun. Today in a restaurant the waitress came up and said how cute we looked. We're fifty-two years old!"

Dressing Alike

As parents of twins, it's hard not to get caught up in the excitement and fanfare of having two. The temptation to dress twins alike, whether they are identical, same-sex or boy-girl twins, is hard to resist. They look so cute, and oh, the attention they garner! I have yet to talk to a set of twins who were not dressed alike at some point in their lives.

"Our mother was really into the twin thing so we dressed alike until we were eighteen. Our joke is that we developed our personalities in spite of her," said Donna DeLozier, now age sixty-one.

Having twins is a source of great pride for parents like me. When they are babies and toddlers, it's hard not to give into the "dressing alike" habit. But for many, the dressing alike went far beyond the boundaries of a special holiday photo. Ella McAraw and Mary McAraw Dianglo, age sixty-nine, remember their mother saying, "As long as I am paying for your clothes, you will dress alike." And so they did until after high school graduation.

Some twins loved it; others hated it. Very few of the twin sets interviewed for this book said they were able to dress independently of each other until they reached a certain age. Twins like Mark and Rick Weaver, age nineteen, had no choice. "We had to dress alike at times. Our mother made us."

"We were always dressed alike," said Retha Fielding. "When we were about six years old, I remember arguing with my twin about what we were going to wear. Finally my grandmother asked me, 'Why don't you just wear whatever you want?' She didn't get it. We were supposed to be dressed alike. We thought it was some unwritten twin law."

Tara Behnke and Christine Rizzo have a similar story. "When we were younger, we looked a lot alike," said Christine. "We even dressed alike in elementary school except for the fact that we wore different colors. It was extremely difficult because people used to think that we were the same person. We had no identity whatsoever. Ironically, now that we are older and don't look alike, people have a hard time believing we are twins."

While some twins may have resented having to wear the same outfits day after day, others genuinely enjoyed it. Jeanne Corfee and Eleanor Killebrew Brown, now in their seventies, dressed alike until they graduated from college. It was fun and they rarely disagreed on what to wear. And—they looked beautiful. Together or separately, they were true showstoppers.

Identities

Past or present, it's hard for twins when they are treated as one person. Nicknamed "the twins," many pairs admit they have had a somewhat confusing childhood. Their parents aren't to be criticized however; this nickname was repeatedly given with love and great pride. They, and other family and community members, meant well and by no means tried to stigmatize the children.

Ella McAraw and Mary McAraw DiAngelo shared their experiences. Ella recalled, "When we were growing up, we were always called 'the twins.' Our brother's name was Jim and it was always 'Jim and the twins.' Nobody ever considered us two people. Today we are still known as the 'McAraw twins.'"

Renee and Rachel Walters, eighteen, know the feeling. They are one of only two sets of twins in their hometown of Blissfield, Michigan. "People always mix us up. They put our names together. They call us Reneechal. We hate it because they can't tell us apart."

"We had an identity crisis about our names," said Kevin Hogan, a thirty-one-year-old twin from Louisville, Kentucky. "Our parents used to introduce us as KeithandKevin all the time. Up until the end of first grade, we thought our name was KeithandKevin or KevinandKeith. When the teacher would ask my name, I would say KevinandKeith."

"We never really thought about it," added Keith. "I just thought that he was KevinandKeith and that I was KeithandKevin and that was it. We always thought we were one. We never distinguished that we were two people."

For Maria and Angela DeCaprio, sixteen, the "twin thing" went beyond the name. It spilled over into other areas—such as gift giving. Maria said, "We always got the same presents for Christmas and everything. It was horrible because if she opened her presents before me then I knew what I was getting. There were no surprises."

Often the confusion over identity can cause a variety of emotions—disgust, anger, and frustration—that are harmful to the twins' relationship with each other. Christine Grimm, twenty-seven, talks about the early years with her identical twin, Angelika. "We were together throughout school except for two years. We had different friends at age nine and couldn't stand each other. We even had a few fistfights. We just got on each other's nerves because we were so close. We really wanted to be treated not as twins but as individuals. People called us the Schwaff twins or just 'the twins.' How do you feel when you are viewed only as a twin? You totally rebel."

Le Melcher is one twin who says his parents went out of their way to help his twin brother, Pete, and him avoid these frustrations. "I think my parents made a concerted effort to help us develop separate identities. They rarely dressed us alike. They tried to encourage different hobbies. Frequently they encouraged us to have different friends. It was almost to the point where we branded our friends as belonging to one or the other. Today we are close, but we are also independent."

School Challenges

"We moved eleven times in eight years when we were growing up, and it was really wonderful to have someone by my side each time at a new school," said Donna DeLozier. "It was not a difficult adjustment, in fact, moving was an adventure for us because we had each other. We didn't *have* to make new friends but we did. We made new friends partly because of being identical and dressing alike, and partly because we moved from California to Minnesota and then to Kentucky, so we had Western accents and we attracted attention."

Jenna Clayton and her sister, Jessi, are still in their early teens. Growing up as twins has been a mixed bag of experiences for them so far. "It has been a lot of fun," said Jenna. "I didn't use to like it, because people would call us 'the twins' when we would rather be called by our own names.

"When we were in first grade we were in the same classes and even dressed alike. Our teacher didn't like us because she was jealous. She was really awful. She wouldn't let us go places together. She used to think we cheated all the time and we didn't even sit by each other. I don't think the teachers were as fair with us as they were with the other kids. When we were younger, even though we were in different classes and would take the same test, we'd get the same answers right and the same answers wrong. Again, sometimes our teachers thought we were cheating."

Linda and Lisa Lieske, thirty-one, were separated by school officials for different reasons. "The teacher in kindergarten didn't think we would be very intelligent, so we should be separated," said Lisa. "But actually we ended up being in the top ten percent of our class when we graduated. I feel like going back and telling our kindergarten teacher that twins aren't stupid. The one nice thing I can say about her is that she made us want to study harder."

"Together—we were always together," said Paul Golde, forty-six, of his childhood experiences with his identical twin, Rick. "In school though, there were a lot of times the administrators would separate us intentionally so that the teachers wouldn't freak out. We were very much alike physically when we were little. The strangest thing was that when we were very small, my brother developed a dime-sized birthmark on his check. In our early teens, it started disappearing. People thought God put it there as a way for people to tell us apart and took it away when we became individuals and didn't need it anymore."

The carefree days of youth turned into more complicated days of high school for many twins. Most had stopped dressing alike but still had the "twin thing" going for them. Some relationships grew stronger while others deteriorated to the point where the twins themselves wondered if the bond could be salvaged. This was the case for Heather Reser and Leslie Rapp, twenty-nine.

"High school was a rough time for us as twins. I think that if we could have, we would have gone to different high schools because we didn't like each other," said Heather. "I don't know what it was. My sister visited me a couple of years ago and said that she hated me in high school. I don't know why."

"Jealousy," Leslie responded.

Heather continued, "We would fight every morning about clothes, hair, and whoever was at the mirror at the time. She would always ask me what to wear and I was like 'Ahhh.' She still does that to this day. Anyway, our friends knew as soon as we got to school we wouldn't be talking to each other. Of course, by second period, we would be best friends and passing notes. We would be our same happy selves. The fights never lasted long."

Jennifer and Penelope Waggoner, twenty-seven, were also together through their young adult years. Jennifer recalled, "Our high school was very small so we were always together because there was no alternative. That made it limited for us to make different friends, so we always had the same group of friends. Then we went to community college together because we commuted back and forth from our home. It was cheaper that way. When we hit college, we both had the same interests so we did that together too. We were able to help each other a lot because we were again in the same classes. We've been enjoying this period of our lives. We know we are not going to be together forever."

The Fifty-Fifty Rule

The environments in which children grow up often contribute to their personalities as adults. Different childhood experiences can translate into strong values and provide the building blocks for becoming responsible, healthy, happy human beings. Such is the case of fifty-one-year-old fraternal twin Donna Smith. Her parents believed in treating their beloved twins as fairly as they possibly could. That meant Donna and her sister received the same gifts, the same chores, and the same amount of love.

It wasn't until later in life when Donna began to do some personal exploration that she identified a pattern in her life that could be directly linked to being a twin. She calls it the "fifty-fifty rule."

Donna remembered, "When we were kids, my mom would get my sister something and I would get something. She always made sure things were very equal in that respect. If we were going shopping, we would each be given the same amount of money to spend. It was very fair. My parents would do everything right down the middle.

"I grew up with and later developed a very strong sense of fairness," Donna continued. "When I began attending personal growth retreats and started recording thoughts and experiences in my journals, this 'fifty-fifty rule' just kept popping up. I recognized that I pull back when I become aware that things— relationships, business situations, and so on—are not equal. When they get out of whack, I take a step back to see if the problem will be corrected. If it isn't corrected, then I get out of the situation.

"For me, the 'fifty-fifty rule' is a good thing. It is a protective mechanism that prevents me from being taken advantage of. It protects me against emotionally damaging relationships. And it protects me from business dealings that have the potential to become financially harmful. I have also come to realize that this strong sense of fairness has made me a real team player in life."

Best Friends, Worst Enemies

"They always fight. They can't even sit next to each other in the same car. If you're going out with them, one has to sit in the front and the other in the back. But they really like being together—you can tell. I'd like to be a twin. I think it would be cool." So says the good friend of one set of identical twin sixteen-year-old girls. It's not uncommon to find stories like this, where the twins know so much about each other that they clash.

Beth Whitaker said of her relationship with her twin Judy, "It's been a different kind of sibling relationship because you share everything. You don't know what it's like not to share things. She's your best friend—your worst enemy. On the other hand, you always have someone with whom you can play jokes on people."

Fortunately there are far more best friends than worst enemies. Most twins relish the closeness they have with their counterpart to the extent that they can't imagine not being a twin.

You have a best friend—someone you can always talk to. Those are the sentiments of twin sisters Betty Burton and Bert Polley, who live together now that their husbands have passed away. They cannot think of a time when being a twin was frustrating or annoying; they have always enjoyed their twinness.

"We have a special bond," said Dennis Jacob, age fifty-two, of his relationship with his twin, Kenneth. "We enjoy being together. We have the same sense of humor, similar tastes and dislikes. Our bond is very intense when we are together—and then there's the humor." Dennis and Kenneth claim no one can make them laugh as much as the other. In fact, they were separated in the third grade because of their ability to know what the other was thinking. Often those thoughts were funny, which lead to the laughter and eventually separation by school officials. To this day, they often laugh simultaneously for no apparent reason.

Sharing the Secrets

Most English dictionaries define the word "trust" with a number of synonyms—confident belief, faith, custody, care, reliance, assurance, hope, dependence. For twins, the word trust can mean all of these things and more. Whether twins celebrate their closeness or are separated by choice, their trust in each other remains strong—and trust is perhaps one of the most important and meaningful qualities a twin relationship can have.

Larry Lynch lost his identical twin brother Garry twenty years ago. He reminisced, "The one thing that I miss the most about Garry is his absolute, unerring trust. No one else comes close to providing the trust that I gave to him and that he gave to me. No one."

Seventy-two-year-old Donald and Edward Makielski live about eight miles apart. They've been together their whole lives, except for when they were in the Navy. "We're best friends," said Don. "I can tell him things that I might not tell other people. I think it's because we have grown up together and have such close interests. I feel like I can confide in him when I can't confide in anyone else."

Heather Reser, twenty-nine, tells her twin Leslie everything—whether Leslie wants to know or not. "She thinks I'm crazy when I tell her very personal things," says Heather. "But I know she won't tell anyone. My secrets stop with her. She is my best friend. She is someone I can rely on through good times and bad. She will always be there for me, no matter what. And I'll be there for her."

Although ten years younger than Heather and Leslie, Jon and Chris have similar feelings. They call each other best friends, and tell each other everything. "I can talk to him about anything I want," said Jon. "I realize that sometimes I should be careful about what

I say because he might get mad, but we tell each other our honest opinions. We tell each other what we think and what we think the other should do."

"We are straight up with one another," added Chris. "Blunt." Both agree that this can sometimes lead to arguments but they also agree that two minutes later they are back to being best friends. They say they have never had a real fight.

Separation Struggles

For many twins, especially those who have shared their childhood as intimately as those in this book, separation is one of the hardest things they experience. So many twins dress alike, attend the same classes, and have the same friends that independence is truly a foreign concept.

Many twins, whether identical, same-sex fraternal or boy-girl fraternal, complement each other as they live their lives. One may have a stronger, more confident personality; another may be more sensitive to the needs of others. Whatever the case may be, when they are separated these two halves of a whole often feel lost and uncertain. Separation can be traumatic. Every twin I have spoken to recognizes one pinnacle moment that explains just how hard separation can be.

There have been many different philosophies about separating twins in school. Some parents choose to keep their twins together in all aspects of their early lives. Others have chosen to separate their children as early as preschool to help them on their journey to becoming individuals. And some twins have been forced to separate because teachers couldn't tell them apart or they were too disruptive when together in class.

Jeannine St. Hilaire and Jackie Gagnon, forty-four, remember the first time they were separated. It was not by choice. "We were in the same classes in Catholic school until the second grade. They had to separate us because we looked so much alike. It was one of the most traumatic events of my life," said Jeannine.

Retha Fielding remembers her defining moment. "We lived in an oil boom town—Snyder, Texas. There were a lot of kids—actually more kids than they had anticipated for school in that town. So they had morning and afternoon half-day classes. They separated us. It was tough that first day. We didn't know where the other one went. Letha was convinced I had been kidnapped. She watched the door all day long to see if she could find me. I got to go home in the afternoon, so I sat by the window, waiting for her to come home. It was the first time we were separated."

Twelve-year-old LaQuintauna and LaQuintearra Travis were separated in school, and that trauma has made them a bit cautious about being separated again. "We were crying because we didn't want to be apart," said LaQuintauna. "It was hard for us then, so we figure it will continue to be hard. We'd like to be roommates in college and are hoping that we can be neighbors when we grow up."

One might think that as twins become older, the desire for independence grows. Perhaps they are tired of their twinness or maybe they just want new life experiences. Still, after spending a lifetime with someone who is almost exactly like you, making the big move can be daunting.

Dona Koelling explained her feelings when she and her sister, Dana Deacon, first parted: "I got mad at her when she moved away and wouldn't talk to her for about six months. I truly felt like my best friend was gone."

Christine Grimm reflects on her first separation with her twin: "We both grew up in Germany and were both adopted. I decided to do something new—to venture out into the world. I left Germany for the United States in 1991. We had a really hard time when I left. We were both nineteen at the time. I remember Angelika would get really mad at me for little things, but it was really because she didn't want me to leave."

Andrew and Anthony Hill also did everything together—they even joined the Air Force together. For them, the "twin thing" worked against them and they were unable to start their new careers at the same time. "We were two weeks apart in boot camp," said Andrew. "The recruiter made a bunch of excuses as to how we couldn't go to basic training together, how we couldn't be stationed together, and how we couldn't get a guaranteed job together. He didn't stay in the recruiting field for very long."

"The first couple of weeks were probably the hardest time of my entire life, up to that point," continued Andrew. "I was trying to deal with the fact that while we were in formation, Anthony was in another flight. He was probably about ten feet away, and I remember seeing him out of the corner of my eye. I wasn't allowed to turn my head. I remember thinking that this is the first time in my life that my brother is within spitting distance of me and I can't even speak to him. It was very hard seeing him there and not being able to go over and say something."

Pearl Bailey once said, "You must change in order to survive."[11] For many twins, little in life stays constant and Pearl Bailey's words ring true for many twins that have separated for one reason or another. However, their emotional survival depends in part on the ability to be with their twin. In the face of change and separation, they may remain connected emotionally and spiritually.

First-time separation happened for Kim Smith and Cheryl Bobelak, forty-three, when they went to different colleges. "Cheryl was very upset because she thought we would never see each other again," said Kim. "We were so used to being together. We had to develop our own identity and new relationships with different people. We didn't do it together. We had to be individuals. Plus, it was like losing your best friend. We cried a lot and talked on the phone a lot."

For Kim and Cheryl, time turned out to be their friend. They were able to adjust to the separation after a while, but still they talked on the phone and wrote lots of letters. Now they've made a choice to be close geographically, and they say that being together again feels wonderful.

Jennifer and Penelope, or Jenny and Penny, separated after college when Penny moved to Cleveland. "I have been here for two years," Penny said, "but I'm contemplating moving back because it is very hard. I don't like being away from her."

Penny says the main reason it's tough is because they are so close. "Moving away from Jenny made me feel lost. I felt lonely and I was sad a lot. The separation made it hard for me to make friends because I had always had her to confide in. It may seem funny, but I really didn't know how to approach making another best friend because Jenny was always just there. When you have a deep connection with somebody, nobody can really replace that. It's better now, but it's not the same."

Joan and Jeannie were separated for about three months. That was about the longest they could endure. "I moved to Tiffin, Ohio, for a job," said Jeannie. "We were in our late twenties. It was tough. Then our dad became terminally ill and I moved back. Fortunately my husband was able to transfer directly into the same type of job he had in Tiffin. It was wonderful to be together again, even under those circumstances."

For Rick and Mark Weaver, it was another story. "Separation was really hard at first, but I got used to it," Rick said. "Mark has always been my role model. He's always been more confident so my confidence level would be slightly lower. I always had my brother there, so people thought we were cool. When I had to become my own person and not just be known as his brother, it was different."

For the Weaver twins, separation turned out to be a positive experience, at least for Mark. "I loved it," Mark said. "For the first time I had my own identity.

Finally I wasn't just known as a Weaver twin. I got out and got to meet so many more people on my own. I lost the buzzing voice that was always in the back of my head. I was finally my own person with my own thoughts."

"I don't want to sound too cruel," said Mark. "I missed him to death and I love him. But we get along better now that we are apart. I am an independent person, and I sometimes get tired of having someone tell me what to wear or how to do my hair. I don't want it to sound like it was all bad. This kid makes me feel great about myself. He's always been there for me even though he has been a bit over-defensive and overprotective of me. If he thinks anyone is trying to say anything bad about me, he is the first one there to make them shut up. He is a great brother and I love him."

For twins like Heather Reser and Leslie Rapp, separation did not turn out to be as traumatic for them as it was for other sets of identicals. "Separation was not hard," said Heather. "We can go for months and months and just talk to each other once a week or so. The wonderful thing is that we can just pick up where we left off. If something exciting happens, we call each other, but otherwise we just live our daily lives."

"This is something a lot of twins would say—it's hard being separated," said Anthony, twin to Andrew, who has been separated for many years due to his brother's career in the armed forces. "But then again, you appreciate the time that you get. There are probably a lot of twins that get together every day and they probably love each other like you wouldn't believe, but put a little bit of separation in that, and it makes the relationship just a little bit more special."

Whether young or old, with a strong connection or not, most twins understand the special gift they have been given. They know that separation may be hard, but it also can help them grow emotionally and spiritually as individuals. With a foundation of love, personal history, and trust, a twin relationship can provide a lifetime of fun, security, and emotional support.

CHAPTER THREE

Perfectly in Tune

Whether you're a husband-and-wife team, a sibling who is very close to a brother or sister, or even a best friend—chances are you have experienced the uncanny and sometimes unsettling ability to communicate effectively without words. You know what another person is thinking. Even my husband and I have the ability to "read each other's minds." He will begin to ask me where something is and before he has a chance to finish his question, I tell him where the object is. Are we that connected? Maybe. But nowhere is the connection and the ability to communicate with or without words more prevalent than in the world of twins.

Secret Language

Much research has been done on "twin speech," which is also called cryptophasia, idioglossia, and autonomous language. In her book *Entwined Lives*, Dr. Nancy Segal defines twin speech as the private gestures, words, and phrases that about 40 percent of twins, most likely identical, develop on their own for communicating with each other.[12] She says this type of speech may be slightly distorted or even unintelligible to anyone outside the twinship.

I have interviewed more than fifty sets of twins and all of them profess some ability to communicate with each other, either in a language of their own or without words at all.

Dennis and Ken Jacob, now in their early fifties, remember when they were small. "We had our own language when we were younger. It was developed after our tonsils were taken out," said Ken. "We thought it would hurt to talk, so we invented our own language that the adults couldn't understand. Oddly enough, we developed the language after we were already speaking. It was probably because of our same wavelength and our ability to understand each other. Today we don't remember any of it."

Connie Wyckoff recalled that she and her twin sister also had an unusual way of communicating. "We had a separate language," she said. "I don't remember much about it except what mother has told me. She said we learned German when we were five, but before that we had our own language. She said when we didn't want anyone to understand us, we always switched to that language, which was our twin language. Our parents just laughed about it, I don't think they took it seriously."

Twin speech can often be elusive. In the case of Tara Behnke and Christine Rizzo, their parents knew about the speech but were never able to prove it. Tara says, "Our parents used to try to tape-record us. Every time we heard them, we stopped. They never got us on tape."

Joan Pahls Notch, an identical twin, explains: "It is very difficult for people to understand that children from the ages of three to six develop their own language. Identical twins do that. Even though it is very normal, it is not socially acceptable. It is a communication that we create between ourselves that nobody can understand. We knew that nobody else could understand, therefore it gave us power, and it was fun."

Even as twins grow older, some still experience the secret language. Take the case of Mark and Rick Weaver. "We grew up together, we never spent more than a day apart, and we watched the same TV programs. Our parents said we would sit at the dinner table and have a conversation, and they wouldn't know what we were talking about. We would mumble to each other. We did it a little bit when we were younger, but that's what we still do today."

Paul Golde communicates with his twin while he

sleeps. Paul said, "My brother and I have been told by others that when we're sound asleep, we will talk to each other in our sleep. At Cub Scouts when we were little, they'd tell us, 'You were just talking away, you kept talking and talking and we told you to shut up and you guys kept talking.' They're general conversations about everyday things—like we're in the garage working on our motorcycles together. We'll say stuff like, 'Hand me the wrench or piston.' Things like that."

As adults, Owen Murphy and his brother, Adam, still have very unique dialogues at times. "We both took German in high school," said Owen. "I took it again in college and ended up living in Germany for a summer. Adam joined me for the last week. Prior to coming over, he tried to learn a few phrases. I tried to teach him some things. Later, when we went to parties, we would use German to talk about girls. And we would use words that we made up when we were seven; they still have meaning and he'll know what I'm saying. It could be a mixture of twin speak and guy talk, but I think they were mostly twin words."

Echoing Thoughts

While we may not be able to catch twins in the act of speaking their unique languages, we can often witness the marvel of unspoken communication between twins. It could be as simple as finishing each other's sentences or claiming a little ESP. But for most twins, it's much more than that.

Many twins admit that the ability to know what each other is thinking is a bit of a nuisance. At age seventy, Bert Polley and her twin sister, Betty, still talk in tandem. "She starts a sentence and I finish it," said Bert, "or vice versa. The whole family gets so mad because they just don't understand us. It happens just because we are so connected."

Tara and Christine explain it differently. "It's not really a feeling. It's just that we know each other and how each other thinks," said Tara. "When something happens or is going on around us, we can just look at each other and automatically know what the other person is thinking. We say a lot of things at exactly the same time."

Jenna and Jessi Clayton say they also know what each other is going to say. "Yes, we finish each other's stories," said Jenna. "And it's not just stories. Sometimes we'll just be sitting there and will start singing the same part of the same song. And sometimes one of us will tell our friends a story, and then the other one will come back and tell the same story. Our friends think it's weird."

After experiencing this for so many years, I asked them if it still surprises them. "Yes," Jenna said. "We just start laughing."

Bill and Bob Lawrence, sixty-four, are also somewhat amused by their connection even though they have had this unique ability to communicate all of their lives. "It happens all the time," said Bob. "It drives people insane. One of us will start a conversation, and then the other will pick it up. We don't plan it that way. We never interrupt each other, but we finish each other's thoughts all the time. We seem to talk in stereo. It's not rehearsed, it just happens."

Bill agreed. "Today," he said, "we share information constantly. A lot of the time, we don't feel like we have to talk. We can relate without talking. It's just natural for us. We can carry on a conversation without saying anything."

Is it a form of Extra Sensory Perception (ESP), are they psychic, or is it just the bond between twins? Science has not been able to answer this age-old question. Twins, however, believe they know the truth.

Jackie Gagnon and Jeannine St. Hilaire have spent forty-four years together and they not only celebrate their twinness but also respect it. "We think alike, even when we are not together," said Jeannine. "It is like we have the same mind—just split in two, and these two halves are walking around in two different places. Often we say things in stereo. We will be in a conversation and say 'wow' together. That is just what talking and thinking in stereo feels like."

Physical Intuition

When twins talk about their bond, their conversations often focus on their ability to know what each other is feeling—both physically and emotionally. The stories are unusual, and not all twins have this ability. Most of the twins I talked to could sense when their twin was going through something, whether it was stress or an emotional burden. About half said they could feel each other's pain or discomfort. As unsettling as that may be, surprisingly it may also serve to comfort twins as they realize that they are strongly in tune with their twin.

"I lost my twin Mike in a car accident," said Lori Neiwert, thirty-eight. "He lost control of his truck, rolled into a lake and drowned. I was on my way to Alaska and in the middle of Canada, I felt him die. I didn't want to know that was what I was feeling but in my heart I knew. I have always said that I had two hearts, his and mine. When mine beat, his answered. That night there was no answer."

It's hard to imagine being so close to someone that

you can actually feel that person's pain. According to many twin sets and a handful of medical associations, the experience of one twin feeling the other twin's pain is called the "twin pain transference syndrome." A layperson, like myself, might break it down into less complex terms and simply call them sympathy pains, but I believe it's much more than that. After talking to twins, it's clear that the twosomes who experience this phenomenon are extremely connected in every way—physically, emotionally, and spiritually. They seem to be acutely in tune with each other's mind and body. They are perceptive, receptive, and very sensitive to the feelings of their twin.

Paul Golde, forty-six, remembered one unusual episode when he and twin, Rick, were young boys. "Our parents recently reminded us of the time we took a holiday drive to South Dakota. We were either eight or nine years old at the time. Rick felt carsick and asked Dad to pull over so he could get out and throw up," Paul recalled. "When he got out of the car, he found that he *couldn't* throw up. The odd thing was inside the vehicle I was throwing up instead. Then Rick got back in the car and said he felt much better."

Bert Polley remembers, "When I was in Okinawa and my sister Betty was pregnant, I knew when she had her baby. We had the same pains."

The connection was even stronger with Donna DeLozier and Dianne Guthrie, now in their early sixties. "When I was in nursing school my father was supposed to meet me and take me to dinner," Donna said. "Instead he called and said Dianne had been in an accident and that he had to go right home. I closed my eyes and I could see blood coming down her face. She had facial injuries and head injuries. I didn't know until hours later exactly what had happened, but I saw it in my mind."

Dianne added, "It's true. Donna can tell when I'm sick or when something bad has happened. I remember how she saved my life when we were about three years old. I had climbed on a shelf and drank cleaning fluid. She was in a closet playing with our mother's shoes and started screaming. Our mother ran to see why she was screaming, but there was nothing wrong with her. My mother then went looking for me and I had already turned blue. Donna's screaming signaled that she intuitively knew something was wrong."

"I believe I also have the ability to feel her pain," said Donna. "One time I had horrible abdominal pains and didn't know why. My mother called me the next morning with the news that Donna had had her baby. I realized my pains had started at the exact time my twin went into labor."

Joan Pahls Notch and Jeannie Van Horn, forty, say these types of occurrences cannot simply be reduced to "women's intuition." They believe it is much more than that. They know when something is wrong with the other. "If I really feel distressed, I will get in my car and drive over to check on my twin. It is sometimes just an overwhelming feeling that is like no other feeling," said Joan. "I remember one time when Jeannie crashed while riding on a go-cart and got a nail stuck in her leg. I felt the pain in my same hip. We were only eight years old, but to this day, it stands out in my mind."

In the course of a lifetime, these experiences become etched in the twins' minds forever. They are powerful memories that not only reaffirm the twin connection but also the twins' love for each other.

Retha Fielding remembered one particular event. "When I was in Europe over the holidays," she said, "I had this horrible feeling that something was seriously wrong back home. My daughter-in-law was pregnant, so I thought there was something wrong with her baby. I called the house only to find out that while the baby was okay, my twin sister, Letha, had pneumonia. The whole time I was gone, I just had a nagging feeling that something was wrong. There was—only with my twin.

"Later Letha was the one to experience this phenomenon. It was the same case with her—an unsettling feeling that something had happened to me. This time it was when my husband was in the hospital. I remember coming home from the hospital and there was a message on the phone. Letha said, 'I know you should be home, I know something is wrong.' And there was. I was worried sick about him and had been under a great deal of stress over his illness. Somehow she just knew that."

Emotional Intuition

From the early days of childhood to the late stages of adulthood, some twins seem to be able to lock into each other's thoughts and emotional well-being—or ill-being, as the case may be. They may have no clues other than just a nagging feeling, or perhaps a quick "stop-me-dead-in-my-tracks" thought. As children, this ability was much more simplistic and fun.

Kim Smith and Cheryl Bobelak remember their early childhood. "It was amazing to us how we could hide things from each other and then know where to find them," said Cheryl. Kim agreed. "As young children I can remember arguing over a Barbie doll or something, and Cheryl hid it from me. I couldn't find it anywhere, so I calmly sat down and thought if I were she where would I hide it? Then I went right to it and found it."

As adults, most twins find this unspoken communication tool to be much more sophisticated—and much more important. Such is the case of Andrew and Anthony Hill. They had gone into the service together but had been separated. It had been tough being apart, but it got even worse when they lost their beloved mother.

"Our mom passed away on Sunday and Andrew was scheduled to leave on an overseas tour to Germany on Monday. When he left, it was the toughest time of our lives. During the next year, I would get depressed—just out of the blue. It would be a beautiful day. There would be nothing wrong, yet I would be feeling really down. I'd feel the overwhelming need to pick up the telephone and call him. I remember saying, 'Buddy, what's going on?' And he told me he had been having a really tough time. For both of us it was just hard not to be able to talk to somebody you care about, and being that far away was even worse. We both missed our mother *and* each other terribly. I really felt his pain."

Anthony added, "We always knew how each other was feeling. We were ten thousand miles away and there was bond between us that told us what the other was experiencing. There have been several times, and I'm sure this happens to everybody, where you pick up the phone and somebody's already there, talking. There have been several times when that's happened to us both."

"That unspoken thing," said Rick Weaver. "We just know what the other is thinking sometimes." Mark and Rick Weaver say they haven't really felt each other's pain but they have felt their bond in other ways. Mark added, "Maybe I'll be thinking of someone that I haven't seen in a long time, and Rick will call me from another state and say guess who I hung out with today? It will be the person I had been thinking about. Those kinds of things happen to us all the time."

Dawn Jordan and Daphne Koenigsberg, forty, have lived extremely parallel lives despite the fact that, up until recently, they haven't lived in close proximity. For a long period of time, they did not have the benefit of being together. It was something they missed dearly, but they managed to live separate, productive lives. Surprisingly, and despite the faraway nature of their relationship, their unspoken communication seems just as strong as that of twins who have never left each other's sides. "Even though we lived in different states, we could always tell when something was wrong with the other," said Daphne. "To this day, we'll call each other up and say, 'are you feeling okay?' We just sense something is wrong because we're feeling weird. We don't understand why we're feeling this way because everything else in our lives might be fine. So we'll call the other one, and sure enough, something is wrong."

Beth Whitaker and Judy Fischer have had the same experience. "We are close. I know when something is wrong, or something is bugging her. I don't have to be near her or even in the same city. I can just tell," said Beth.

Linda and Lisa Lieske, thirty-one, are not ashamed or embarrassed to say they need each other. In fact, they believe they are lucky to have such strong feelings. Linda said, "We talk on the phone every day. We don't miss very often. And we see each other pretty much every weekend."

Lisa added, "I think it is a need. I need to find out what is going on—did I miss out on anything in her life?"

Jeannie Van Horn knows that feeling all too well. "Even though I have Joan's emotional, mental, and spiritual support, it's nice having a physical being around and available, even if you don't need it. It's almost like even though you don't have a headache, it's nice to have aspirin in the house. I don't get actual pain, but I do feel a deep-seated yearning for her sometimes. It is very difficult to explain. It is just a desire to know. It's also very disturbing sometimes because you can't always get your answers when you want them."

Retha Fielding reflected, "Letha has been my security, my comfort. Especially when I think back to when I went through my divorce. And then for her, when one of her children was injured very badly. We were like lifelines for each other. I was in New Hampshire and she was in Texas, yet I really needed her. We kept each other going. It's much harder for me to watch her have those painful experiences than to go through them myself. That's the need and the bond."

Twins are among the few who are blessed with a special ability to communicate through encrypted language, unspoken communication, thoughts and dreams, and shared spirituality. Twins themselves will tell you that the joy of having one person who truly understands you physically, emotionally, and spiritually is one of the most precious and satisfying gifts in their life.

CHAPTER FOUR

Joyful Twinness

"Guilty until proven innocent." That's a line every identical twin may want to include in his or her arsenal of retorts when accused of playing tricks on unsuspecting singletons. Most people automatically assume that twins love to play tricks, whether the tricks are on parents, teachers, friends, or lovers. After all, it's so easy to do—simply exchange identities and no one will be the wiser.

Twins are routinely asked if they have ever purposely switched places with each other to get out of a chore or a school assignment, to avoid dating someone creepy, or to get out of a sticky situation. The answer may surprise you. Most of the twins interviewed for this book had one or two stories they admitted to, but most said they really didn't live their lives that way. They were too busy trying to be perceived as their own person.

The truth is that not all twins play tricks on people. Sometimes people just get confused or may not know the twins as well as they think they do. They may be overconfident in their ability to identify identical twins. The end result is that people get fooled through no fault of their own. The most common experience is simply a case of mistaken identity, which can start at birth. Who can fault parents when their babies look so much alike?

Cheryl Bobelak talks about her parents' dilemma. "When Kim and I were babies, we were very identical," Cheryl said. "My mom was the only one who could truly tell us apart. Once, after giving us a bath, we had our names pinned to our T-shirts and she got us mixed up. My father told her she was wrong. Our parents argued for about a week and finally took us back to the hospital. Our mother had our footprints redone to prove that she was right. And she was right. She could tell us apart by our voices, our footsteps, any little thing. She didn't even have to look at us."

Mistaken Identity

Others have not been so talented or lucky as Cheryl's mother when it comes to telling twins apart. Mistaken identity is generally the biggest culprit when it comes to people being fooled by a pair of twins. No matter how well family and friends may think they know a set of twins, they often set themselves up for confusion and doubt. Spouses are no exception. No one is immune from pinching the wrong twin or whispering in the wrong ear.

"People play tricks on themselves," said Helen Underwood. "Twins don't usually play tricks. Somebody will see my twin, Ellen, down the hall and then I'll walk up and join him or her. They'll laugh and say 'Oh, you stop that! Why do you all do that?' That's the way it is. And we didn't do a thing!"

Jeannie Van Horn and Joan Pahls North say people really are the cause of their own angst. "What is really interesting is when I go into a department store and people who do not know talk to me as if I were Joan. And then I'll meet someone else and talk about having a twin and they respond with a 'sure you do' retort. It's as if they don't believe you. Why would someone make up a twin?"

Dona Koelling and Dana Deacon's mistaken identities have actually caused problems with normal everyday activities. "When we first got our driver's licenses we were eighteen," said Dona. "The state of Illinois had us recorded as one person because our names were alike. We have the same middle initial and of course our birthdays are the same. Our Social Security numbers are one number apart.

"Three years later we went to get our licenses renewed and they said no; there was only one of us. I had to put my middle name first so I could get my own driver's license number. Our credit reports are always a mixed bag—some elements are mine and some are hers. Lastly, when Dana had gall bladder surgery at the hospital where I worked, they put Dona (my name) down and billed *my* insurance company. My insurance company couldn't figure it out, so it eventually paid her bill."

Dennis and Ken Jacob, fifty-two, remember their military days. "When we were in the Air Force together we did not introduce ourselves as twins," Dennis recalled. "Ken was working with a guy who didn't know he had a twin brother on base. The man was driving around and waved at Ken. Then he spotted me walking into a building. When he found out Ken had a twin, he admitted to wondering how he could get to that building so fast, and wanted to know his shortcut."

Ken added, "Another time I had walked into the bathroom. An instant later, my brother came walking down the hall. A very confused acquaintance of ours, who happened to be standing in the hall at the time, couldn't understand how that could have happened— what had he missed."

Sometimes people just can't help but assume that they know whom they are talking to. After all, identical twins—unless they are side by side and there is some physical differentiation—are incredibly difficult to tell apart. It's even harder if a person doesn't even know the twin is a twin.

Judy Fischer, thirty-seven, remembered, "I was in a store one time and a woman just started talking to me as if she knew me well. I didn't know her at all. After about five minutes I finally told her she must know my sister, Beth Whitaker. We had teachers do the same thing all the time."

Beth said, "I have had relatives from Judy's husband's side of the family talk to me thinking I was she. And then there were the times when I've had her walk into my workplace and the people there would think she was I. Last year we were working in the same nursing home but I was on one side of the building and she on another. One day state inspectors arrived. They had seen us, separately, in different locations but at about the same time. Finally we both happened to walk up at the same time and one inspector realized we were twins. She—and her coworkers—thought one of us had been running all over the place."

Kim Smith and Cheryl Bobelak had the same problem in school. Kim recalled, "I had an English teacher in high school who stopped Cheryl in the hallway and asked, 'Can I have permission to read one of your papers to some of my classes?' Well, Cheryl didn't have that teacher and so she said, 'No, I don't know what you're talking about.' He said, 'Well, you're Kim.' She said, 'No, I'm not.' And he wouldn't believe it. He went to every faculty member trying to get validation that she was I. All the teachers knew we were twins except him. He was so embarrassed. We had been there four years!"

Of course, mistaken identity can have its advantages and disadvantages. Calvin and Keith Robinson, now forty-four, know all too well how the line "I'm not my brother's keeper" may not always work, especially when it comes to twins. Calvin said, "If your twin brother owes somebody some money and the person doesn't know that you're a twin, he is going to come looking for you! He thinks you're the same person."

On the other hand, mistaken identity has also worked in Calvin and Keith's favor. Keith remembered, "I was out on bond and part of the agreement was that I was not supposed to leave the base. At the time I was in the service. Well, I left the base and wouldn't you know it, the police showed up looking for Calvin and found me instead. They ran my name and before I knew it I got called back into court for a bond revocation. When we got into court, my twin was sitting on one side of the courtroom and I was sitting by my lawyer. When my lawyer got a state trooper on the stand, he asked him if he was sure that I was the man he saw. The state trooper said he was sure. My lawyer said, 'That's not my client; this is my client.' I stood up and my brother stood up and everyone, including the judge, did a double take. That kept me from going back to jail."

Tricks

Usually one of the first questions asked of twins is if they play tricks on people. It seems like the perfect thing to do. And why not? After all, twins can look and sound exactly alike. If they dress alike, that's even better. As a singleton, I can think of all the possibilities—school, dating, jobs, sports. What an opportunity!

When asked if he played a lot of tricks on unsuspecting victims, Keith Robinson replied, "Not really. We got in trouble a few times but not on purpose. One day my twin, Calvin, was out of school. I went to class and my teacher sent me over to where Calvin was supposed to be. His teacher thought he was late. Another time I almost got fired from a job. Calvin came to visit me on his lunch hour and the president of my company saw him riding around in the parking lot. The president then went to see if I was on the time clock, which I was. He told my supervisor to fire me because I was supposedly on the time clock while riding around the parking lot. We finally got it straightened out and I got to keep my job."

Owen Murphy and his brother, Adam, say they really didn't play tricks or date the same girls either. Owen said, "I can think of only one time that we tried to fool the teacher. It was in the eleventh grade and it was hard because the teachers knew both of us. I asked the teacher if I could go to the bathroom, then I went into the hall and I saw my brother. Adam walked back into my classroom instead of me. The students knew it was Adam, but the teacher didn't pay any attention. We have always placed an emphasis on getting people to laugh. He decided he would ask the teacher some dumb questions to make the kids laugh even more. I walked in, and she didn't realize that both of us were now in the room. I sat in the back and put my head on a book. The funny thing was that Adam's questions were so dumb, it not only made the class laugh, but it also made me look dumb, which was his playful intent. She scolded him and said, 'Had you paid attention in eighth grade, you would know this!' She finally caught on.

"The only other real trick happened about two years ago. My dad was having a surprise birthday party. We were trying to beat him back to the house and of course, we were pulled over for speeding. Adam was driving, and I was in the passenger seat. He had several points against his driving record and I had none. I gave him my driver's license but wasn't too happy about taking the rap for him. When the officer saw that I had a clean record, he said, 'Your record indicates that you are not a bad driver, tell your dad to have a happy birthday.' He believed us! We were amazed."

At the age of sweet sixteen, Susan and Sarah Borisuk use their likeness to have some real fun. Sarah said, "My sister, Susan, and I were at a church event. I was talking to these guys on one side of the church and she was on the other side. They thought we could bend spoons or something. They asked me if we could send brain waves. I gave her a look from across the church and she started coming over. I told the boys that I didn't do anything. She was horsing around like she knew what she was doing. Boy, were they surprised."

Le and Pete Melcher say they didn't have to rely on mistaken identity to play tricks, especially when the victim was so primed. "Some girl at a bar would ask if we could really send a number back and forth," said Le. "She would whisper a number in his ear and I would get kicked twice under the table. As I recall, she was infatuated with both of us. It was a very effective way to meet girls. I don't know what we would have done if she would have whispered seventy-eight!"

There are a few twin pairs that admit to having a lot of fun—in every category—when it comes to playing tricks. Dennis and Kenneth Jacob played a few on girls while in their teens. Dennis said, "We have switched dates. When we were either fifteen or sixteen, we would go into the bathroom, come out, and go to the other girl. We don't think the girls ever really figured it out."

Don and Ed MaKielski also pulled a few fast ones. Don remembered," "In high school, I thought I would do my brother a favor by getting him a blind date, so I asked two girls out for the same night. I asked one girl to a dance and the other to a football game. Ed took one of the young ladies to the game and they chatted famously until the first half was over. When she said, 'I wonder what Ed is doing tonight?' Ed said, 'You should know, you're sitting next to him!' She was so confused, she turned to two perfect strangers behind her and asked, 'Do you know who I'm with?' They thought the poor girl was drunk!"

Ed added, "We also played tricks on our teachers in college. When I wanted to go home on a weekend, he took my Friday classes for me."

Don explained, "My class was from 9 to10 and his was from 10 to 11. So I stepped out of class and back in. Unfortunately Ed forgot to tell me that his class had broken up into five discussion groups, so I had to guess which group he was in. So I picked the one I thought was his and sure enough it was the one he had taken. I knew him pretty well. I just pretended I was him and took part.

"One other time in college, I had an English class in room 45 and he had a class in room 47. Boy, did we give this poor teacher the nightmare of her life. Each morning we stood outside my door, room forty-five, and chatted. One time we came in from the other side of the building and stood outside Ed's class door, which was room forty-seven. The teacher walked right past us into room forty-nine. She finally looked up and didn't see a familiar a face. Because of us, she had entered the wrong door. She swore that we had tricked her on purpose."

Uncertainty over true identities is just a fact of life for twins. In fact, there's a children's book called *Double Trouble* that continually asks the question, "Was it was Tim or was it Jim?" Sometimes twins can't even count on mistaken identity. That was the case for Kevin Hogan, thirty-one, and his brother Keith. "We had a baby-sitter at the house, and my brother decided he wanted to go back and play around with the furnace," said Kevin. "He tried to blow out the furnace with an aerosol can. Instead he blew out the pilot light. Then he wanted me to help him light the furnace. I said no, but when he got caught he told our mother that I blew the light out with him. He won't tell the truth to this day." Keith added with a grin, "I figure if I'm going to get it, he's going to get it too!"

Twelve-year-old LaQuintauna and LaQuintearra Travis have also played their share of tricks on people—mostly friends. "When we first meet them we play tricks, but after a while they get to know us," said LaQuintauna. LaQuintearra agreed, "Sometimes we like to get on the phone and pretend to be each other. Then I tell them, 'Now I know all your secrets.' My sister does the same."

Whoops!

Twins will tell you that mistaken identity is bad enough, but when you combine it with love and romance, the recipe can be dangerous. In marriage, it's even worse. Many twins have unwittingly been called liars, cheaters, and cads! They have been accused of everything from pinching, to philandering. And it's not their fault. Really.

Joan Pahls Notch recalled, "Jeannie and I both were going to Kent State University. She was majoring in special education and I was working on my nursing degree. On campus, there is a bus stop close to the Student Center. I remember one time a guy from Jeannie's class and I were waiting for the bus. This guy kept poking at me. He teased, "Is there a problem Jeannie?" And I said, 'I'm not Jeannie.' Right when I said that, Jeannie arrived, and he was so embarrassed."

Dennis Jacob said, "There have been times that people have thought I was having an affair. One time I was in a restaurant with my wife, Rachel, and a woman that knew my twin and his wife very well walked up to me and said, 'Hi Ken, where's Karen tonight?' She thought she had caught Ken having an affair. So I said, 'I suppose my twin brother is home with his wife this evening.' And she just turned scarlet. That has happened a couple of times.

"People simply make assumptions. My wife and I walked into church and we immediately heard mumbling and whispering. We later found out that nearly the entire congregation thought Ken had dumped

Karen and walked into church with his new girlfriend."

Ken added, "Our wives are actually very good sports about it. In fact one time during an elevator ride at the University of Akron, my wife, Karen, was talking to one of the professors and the professor mentioned my name. It came out in the conversation that I was a twin. What a relief to the professor—he thought that Dennis was having an affair with Karen."

Is That You or Me?

You may be shocked to learn that even twins themselves can get confused. Chuck Szopo, twenty-three, lovingly rats on his brother: "Last week at the hotel, Mike was washing his hands, saw his reflection, and had a conversation with the mirror."

Ellen Starr and Helen Underwood, age fifty-eight, admit, they, too, have had their moments of confusion. "One day I was in a department store, and I didn't know that my twin was in the department store as well. We were going down separate aisles, I looked over and saw her, but I thought I was looking into a mirror. We were in the cosmetic department and you know how many mirrors they have there. I looked into 'the mirror' and thought to myself, I'm not wearing that outfit! I backed up, and at the same she backed up. She said, 'Oh, Ellen!' and I said, 'Oh, Helen!' Talk about a good laugh."

Making the Grade

One of the biggest temptations for twins, hands down, has got to be in academics. After all, if one twin is strong in a subject and the other twin is strong in another subject, the logical thing to do would be to help each other out—in whatever way you can. Dona Koelling and Dana Deacon knew this trick well. Dona reported, "In high school, Dana could not get out of her English class. She kept failing her test, so I had to go in and take her exams for her. We switched boyfriends in high school, switched classes. They never really knew who we were."

Jenny and Penny Waggoner fell victims to the same temptations on more than one occasion. Jenny recalled, "We were both preparing to take a major exam. The class was Food and Beverage Cost Control. I remember there was a lot of accounting. I was stronger in that area so I took Penny's driver's license and ID and sat in the front row. I was a little nervous. Needless to say, she got an A in the class."

Penny added, "We always traded places on the phone. Our voices are very much alike. It was great because we could switch off if we didn't want to talk to a certain person. Another time, and this is bad, but if I wanted to call in sick for work and I just couldn't make the call, Jenny would call for me instead. She would say, 'this is Penny.'"

Even eighty-seven-year-old twins Marie Queen and Wynona Newberry acquiesce that they had gotten some mileage out of being twins. "One year in high school, we switched classes," said Marie. "I am not good at Biology and she's not good at Gym so we switched. I sat in for her and she for me. Nobody could tell. We didn't even switch clothes that day; they just didn't know." Wynona added, "It was fun. Our friends knew, but we had to inform others in the classes so they wouldn't tell. It worked."

Keith and Kevin Hogan, thirty-one, also had lots of twin fun in elementary school. "I remember one time in the first grade my brother, Keith, was sick and not going to school," said Kevin. "So I went to school as Keith not realizing that I was the one who was going to be counted absent. I spent the whole day in his classroom, but the teacher figured it out by the end of the day. The teacher called home and I knew I was going to get a whooping, but my mom just laughed and laughed."

Keith continued the story. "When Kevin got home the phone was ringing and he kept saying, 'Momma, Momma, who was that?' She said the teacher's name, and he ran out of the room and cried and cried. She was mad at first, but then all she could do was laugh."

The stories go on and on. It was easy for twins to switch clothes and classes. It was easy for them to take tests for one another, by simply memorizing each other's social security numbers. Even at the ripe old age of ten, Alysha and Alexandria Chmielewski Schall have played a few. "It's really fun to try and trick people. In third grade, we once traded clothes in the locker room after gym class and we switched desks, and nobody knew. Then someone finally told the teacher."

Sometimes twins got caught right off the bat. It was the personality that often gave them away. Jeannine St. Hilaire said, "In high school, when we didn't have classes together, we switched. But Jackie was more of a participant in her classes, so when I went into her classes the teachers knew right away I wasn't her. They knew right away because I wasn't participating. They didn't count it as a day we missed; that was a good thing."

"High school was great," said Anthony Hill. "When Andrew and I started tenth grade we decided that we wanted to spice things up a bit, so we went ahead and started switching classes. The first couple of months, a lot of the teachers found out about it and they were making bets in the teachers' break room at lunch trying to figure out if the Hill twins were switching that day. Have they switched today or are they going to come into your class tomorrow? There were quite a few that did catch us, but it was a lot of fun. They were in it for the fun of it too.

"There were some interesting times. I took Spanish class for Andrew, and I didn't speak Spanish at all. And because we are mirror twins, we write with different hands. He's right-handed and I'm left-handed. It was always a question of whether the teacher would notice if one of us was writing with the wrong hand today."

Christine Grimm remembered, "When we were really young, Angelika and I played tricks. The kids always knew who we were and what we were doing, but the teachers didn't. When we competed in gymnastics, our trainer would ask us sometimes to compete as one person. She was better than me on the balance beam and I was best doing the floor routines and the vault. Because we competed as one, we won a lot."

Twin tricks are as diverse as the twin sets themselves. Twins don't deny that they have had their fair share of fun pulling the wool over the eyes of a teacher, boyfriend, or coworker. They also laugh at the fact that they have fallen victim to episodes of self-mistaken identity. In the end, it's safe to say that most twins enjoy *being* twins and all the fun and games that go along with it.

Twin Sister Sisters

When I was at Twinsburg, I met identical twin sisters—Sister Rosemary and Sister Jane Frances. At sixty-nine years young, they were full of great tales. Often, even these very pure ladies of the church were accused of being mischievous twins who liked to play tricks. They, of course, were innocent.

"It has been a wonderful, happy experience," said Sister Rosemary. "We have so many happy memories as twins it is hard to really choose stories to tell. Probably the most fun part about being twins is the whole mistaken-identity aspect. People who met one of us in our jobs at the different churches where we worked or taught school would often run into Sister Jane Frances say, 'Sister Rosemary, why didn't you tell me you had a twin?' And vice versa. That happens so often.

"I remember when Sister Jane Frances worked in Layefette, Indiana, for seventeen years. I was teaching school here in the Cleveland area and then she came back home and was living at the Mother House in Bedford. One day she called me and said, 'I'm tired of telling people that I'm not Sister Rosemary.' All the years I was meeting people and making friends and then when she came home they were confused and surprised, not knowing that there were two of us. This has happened all our lives.

"We didn't really play tricks on people on purpose," said Sister Rosemary. "Not really. Not that I remember. We are usually the victims of people playing tricks on themselves. I remember when we started college; we both entered the convent and joined the church community at the same time. When we were in the first year of college, one of our professors became kind of angry because he couldn't tell us apart. He said that he wanted one of us to wear a chain and a medal so he would know who was who. Mother Superior gave Sister Jane Frances the chain and medal to wear outside on her dress. The professor then said, 'Well my God, now I don't remember which one of them is wearing the medal!' We have had really funny things like that happen to us.

"Once we had a professor in class who would sit at his desk and have the students read out loud from the textbooks," she continued. "He seldom looked up and after one person read, he would call in a loud voice, 'Next' and the reading would continue. Sister Jane Frances and I sat beside each other. The first time I stopped reading and she took over, the professor shouted, 'Next!' Our voices sounded identical. One of the students shouted back, 'It is the next one; they're twins!' He was embarrassed and most unhappy."

"And then there are the birthdays," said Sister Jane Frances. "When we were visiting our family back home in Youngstown, Taylor, our grandniece, laid down on her Grandmother's kitchen floor and began singing, 'Happy birthday to you, happy birthday to you, happy birthday, Sister Jane Frances'—and then spontaneously added a second verse, 'Happy birthday to the other one...' She always expects to see both of us together but recognizes us as two separate people.

The Sisters are independent, yet remarkably alike. They are identical in so many ways that it often confuses even them. They say that they really get puzzled when they look at their notes and papers from college. The handwriting is so close that they can't tell which document belongs to whom. They don't seem to mind the confusion, though.

"When you don't tell people that you are a twin, they are shocked when they see you together," continued Sister Jane Frances. "It has been fun! The receptionist at our convent went on vacation last summer and we had a young lady take her place. I signed out to go to Akron. Later she became very confused. She thought I had changed my mind about leaving when Sister Rosemary signed out to leave for Wickliffe. She had no idea there were two of us."

"Probably the most interesting story about the chaos we have caused is medical in nature," Sister Rosemary added playfully. "We have a nurse, Tammie, who comes to visit us. She takes our blood pressure and checks on the elderly, retired Sisters. After she had been with us for about four months, I asked Tammie if I could see my medical card and she showed me my sister's. I then realized that all the time Sister Jane Frances and I visited the clinic, Tammie thought we were one person. She had never seen us together. She had our blood pressure readings mixed together on one card. I remember her expression when I asked, 'Do you know that there are two of us?' Her face dropped and I thought she was going to faint!"

The twin sister Sisters seem to be the victims of mistaken identities more than their fair share. In addition to not being able to get their medical information recorded properly, they have also been denied their constitutional rights. Sister Rosemary reminisced about a past election day. "When we vote, our names appear next to each other in the registry because of our April 24th birthdate. I recall the November day I went to vote in the presidential election and was denied my right because, according to the clerk, I had already voted that morning! She did not believe I had an identical twin and that we were born on April 24, 1931. Someone had neglected to enter my name into the registry. Sadly, I did not vote in the presidential election that year."

The ladies agree—you never know what price you'll pay for being a twin, but they also agree that they would not trade the experience of being a twin for anything in the world.

CHAPTER FIVE

The Competition

Competition among siblings, though often subtle, is a normal part of family life. Few families, except for those with only one child can escape some sort of sibling rivalry. Brothers and sisters often compete for everything from love and attention, to praise and rewards. Often the competition is not openly recognized or acknowledged but instead subtly permeates family dynamics. Parents don't realize, for example, that when they offer a reward to the child without any cavities, they have created a situation that can be perceived as some sort of unspoken contest among siblings.

Twins are no exception to the competition rule. Most will admit they are very competitive, and their competitiveness extends to sports, school, business, romance, and other areas of life. With twins, it's easy to identify three distinct patterns of competition. Sometimes there is great competition between siblings, with the parents playing a key role in spurring it on. Often this kind of competition plays a negative role in the twins' relationship with each other and in family dynamics as a whole. In other cases, the competition is much more positive as twins use competition to improve their own skills and knowledge. In some cases, competition morphs into teamwork. And then there are the twins who feel they are not competitive at all. Ellen Starr and Helen Underwood feel that way. "There was no reason to be competitive," said Ellen. "We never thought about it. We are the same."

Kim Smith and Cheryl Bobelak say they aren't competitive with each other either, though they had to think long and hard before answering. When asked if they are competitive, Kim commented, "We just enjoy doing things together. It wasn't who could get the better grade or who could be better at doing something. We just liked doing things together, so there really was, and is, no need to compete."

Twin Rivalry

Kim and Cheryl were two of the lucky ones. Competition was not something that consumed them or even something they thought about. At age forty-three, they say they are still able to live their lives in harmony. Other twins have not been so fortunate.

"My parents used competition as a way to motivate us," said Connie Wyckoff, fifty-eight, when talking about growing up as a twin. "That was very important to our folks. If one of us got an A and the other got a B, my parents would make us feel that the only one loved was the one who got an A. It was a difficult way to be raised. My folks and I talked about it recently and they said they didn't know it was negative at the time. When we were growing up, no one gave you a class on how to rear twins. They did the best they could."

"We were very competitive and still are," said Paul Golde. "We were competitive about our grades, who could have a girlfriend first, then motorcycle racing. When we started racing motorcycles, there was definitely no love lost between us on the track even though we raced for the same shop. (Rick was faster though.) When I wanted a truck first, Rick said he wanted one too. I said, 'You can't have a Mazda pickup, get something else!' In the end, we both bought the same Mazda pickup truck from the same dealer on the same day. Thank goodness one of us chose red and the other yellow.

"We competed in so many ways—whoever got one thing or did something, the other was right behind— like with paper routes or the time I got a job at the Sizzler and then he did too two weeks later. It was almost comical because we tried to outdo each other, but most of the time we ran neck and neck. We bought the same trucks, took the same regional occupation program at high school. He got into the Plexiglas industry and I got into the fiberglass industry. Same but different. Then I started working for a big motorcycle company. A couple of years into it, he asked me if I could get him a job there. I thought to myself when is this going to end? But we were mature enough to laugh about it. We worked at the same company for three or four years. It's kind of funny now."

Susan and Sarah Borisuk, sixteen, also admit competition plays a key role in their relationship. "Yes. We are very competitive," said Susan. "We were in the same gym class this year and we were really, really competitive." Sarah added, "Once we were playing a game called Ultimate Frisbee. The score was tied and my sister caught the Frisbee in the end zone right as the teacher blew the whistle. They won. After that Susan was right in my face, flicking the Frisbee in my face. We had a huge fight, and they had to hold me back. We got over it. We always do."

Maria and Angela DiCaprio, also sixteen, have found themselves in somewhat similar situations, except that the focus of the competition has been on practically everything including academics. Maria said, "Angela is better at school that I am, but I'm better at everything else. We get mad at each other easily. If one wins, the other is always mad. It's important to each of us that we win."

Competition between twins has the potential to spill over into everyday activities. Little routine tasks can easily turn into major sporting events where victor takes all. Sometimes it's tough living like that.

Linda Houk and Laura Fryman, forty-two, say they were very competitive as well. "We didn't do sports but competed in other things like vying for a friend's time, our time alone, or getting the car by ourselves," said Laura. "We competed for more everyday-type of things."

When asked if there was competition between them, Mark and Rick Weaver, nineteen, answered with one word: "Definitely." Mark said, "We were competitive in everything—sports, school, girls. Anything that got us attention, we were quite competitive about." Rick added, "Horrible, the competition was horrible. I get jealous of him when he beats me or is better than me, but at the same time, he's like a role model to me. The competition between us is both good and bad."

A Healthy Dose of Competition

Winning is a great feeling, no matter who you are and no matter what you do. Everyone enjoys the thrill of the adrenaline rush when you cross the finish line or ace the final Jeopardy question. Young or old, there is great personal pride in accomplishing something of merit. With a number of twin sets, though, there is another element that accompanies victory and cannot be ignored—the feelings of your twin. Robert South, a famous 17th century English clergyman, once said, "Defeat should never be a source of discouragement but rather a fresh stimulus."[15] For many twins, that statement rings true. Competition can play a very positive role in the development of twins, especially as they strive to enhance their personal growth.

Kevin and Keith Hogan were very competitive growing up, and at age thirty-one, they still are. Kevin commented, "We are competitive, but we are competitive in a way that I don't care if he wins. I am happy for him. If he makes a lot of money—more money than me—I am happy as I can be. And then if he beats me in something, the next time we go out I am going to try extra hard to beat him."

Keith added, "We don't do it to be competitive against each other, we do it just to try to make ourselves better. If I lose I'm not going to get mad about it, but the next time I'm going to try harder to better him. That went for sports and for school, and now for many of the activities in our adult lives."

Sometimes competition just happens. Twins find themselves in small towns with small schools and small teams, or they may develop an equal interest in a sport, musical instrument, hobby, or pastime.

"We ran track in high school and college so we had to compete," said Don MaKielski of the competitive athletic relationship with his brother. Ed added, "We tried to beat each other, but we didn't really care who won. Our coaches liked the fact that they had twins on the team. We gave them not one, but two people who knew what to do, and we pushed each other to do better and better."

Dean and David Jensen, twenty-three, remember their college wrestling days. Dean recalled, "We both wrestled at the college. My brother had lost to this one guy the time before and the time before that, so the coach made us both cut five pounds the day before the next match so I could wrestle the guy instead. And I won. I kept rubbing it in because it was a major decision. I beat him by eight points. I teased David, 'You couldn't get the job done.' We were competitive, sometimes in a playful way, but not always. Fortunately we never really had the direct head-to-head competition."

Patrick and Mike Halpin, forty-four-year-old identical twins, had the same success in their athletic careers, only the competition between the two eventually evolved into a very complementary partnership. Pat said, "In football, Mike was the quarterback and I was the end. We would work out our plays out in the street in front of our house. The coach knew this and would always send in a play using the words 'Hit your brother.' Then Mike would simply tell me to hit the manhole. We had a lot of fun."

Having a lifelong companion to test the waters with was a great thing for Owen Murphy, age twenty-four. It forced his brother, Adam, and him to explore the unexplored. "Competition was not a bad or unhealthy thing for us because we branched off into trying new things we might not have tried," Owen recalled. "Even if we both had roughly the same skill set—say at Ping Pong, snow-boarding, or waterskiing—he'd be better at one aspect of the sport than me, and vice versa. For example, with waterskiing, I would try new tricks, but he could compete in the slalom. We truly complemented each other and grew because of it."

Mike and Chuck Szopo, twenty-three, exemplify a twin's ability to bring out the best in the other. Since they were small, they have run neck and neck in just about everything they do. Mike said, "We were in the same classes. Unbelievably my grade point average was a mere .02 better than his was. We competed scholastically. Absolutely. We always chided each other when one got a better grade. It was like a footrace. I'd get a better grade and then he would get a better grade. It made us better students. We studied together. We are a good team.

"I think because we are competitive, we—as a team—are a very attractive package to potential employers. We were both recently hired to work for the GPO in Washington, D.C. Companies know that we will do a good job because we inspire each other."

Jeannie Van Horn is a savvy businesswoman who realizes that being a twin can often have its advantages. She explained, "Because of that competitive factor many companies are welcoming twins. They know about the competitive factor and they know twins will always do a great job. Companies are smart. They already know twins love each other because they may be living together and because they want a job together. They understand that most twins get along very well. The bonus is that twins who work together may not leave because of their loyalty to one another."

At any rate, many twins believe that a little friendly competition never hurt anybody. Competition can be done subtly; it can be kept between the two of them. Growing up, Jeannie and twin, Joan, used their competitive natures to help one another in a way that had a critical impact on their lives. Joan said, "Through school we were competitive scholastically. We worked together, but we still competed for grades. That only lasted through elementary school. It definitely made us better students."

Jeannie added, "In fact, it made us excellent students—but we weren't always so good. One thing that's interesting is that when we were younger than kindergarten age, I had some minor speech and developmental drawbacks. I wasn't quite up to par with Joan and she wanted me to be. Once I caught up it, we became competitive. I think that in the back of our minds, we were just helping each other."

Jackie Gagnon and Jeannine St. Hilaire, forty-four, say their competition is playful in nature, but at the same time, it produces some pretty impressive results. "Ultimately we don't have a competitive issue between us. It's more like a game, and it's fun. Out of a class of 457 students, we graduated number 99 and 100. We were that close in our grades. We did everything together. We did our homework together. We hung out together. We still do when we can."

When you talk to twins, the subject of competition

never fails to come up. It seems it is such an inherent part of their lives. My favorite commentary on competition belongs to Le Melcher, a very articulate and energetic twin who loves his brother Pete dearly. Today, they live side by side. The competition between the two is aggressive and seemingly unending. Still, through every example of one-upmanship, their friendship remains strong.

"We are very competitive," said Le. "If we're skiing together, it's going to be a hazard for somebody. Driving, business, we compete in everything. I made partner at the law firm where I worked. He was in a muck, so he quit his job at a bank, went out, bought a company, and turned it around to make a good amount of money. A few months later, I quit my job at my law firm, went out, bought a company, and did the very same thing. We are very competitive.

"For us, it's sort of like playing chess or tennis with someone you like. The amount of time we give advice or help each other in the quest to become successful is phenomenal. We strive to become as good as each other, and as a result, we become better.

"It wouldn't do to beat him in a business deal if he wasn't doing his best. We're both competitive, but we both would not want to succeed if the other was doing poorly and vice versa. It's sort of like going to the

Olympics. If your training mate didn't make it, it just wouldn't be the same."

Karen Brown, age thirty-two, and her identical twin, Kim Bellnier, were very competitive as children, but as they blossomed into adulthood, their feelings changed. In fact, they tried very hard not to be competitive, especially when it came to very special events in their lives.

"I actually shared my first pregnancy with my twin," said Karen. "I had fertility problems and it took a lot longer for me to get pregnant than expected. That was a big struggle for my sister because she and her husband had wanted to plan for their second child.

"She had thought that I would be 'done' by the time they wanted another. She was concerned about becoming pregnant before I did or even sharing a pregnancy with me because this was to be my first. She did not want to take away from my special moment. Most sisters would not even think of this as an issue, but with twins, having shared every material item and emotional and physical milestone in your life, you think about it. She did not want to 'steal my thunder.' I suppose it's fair to say we have become more sensitive and compassionate toward each other as adults.

"As fate would have it, I became pregnant with my first child at last, and within a few weeks, my twin found out she was actually pregnant with her second. I was happy for her but admit that I felt some disappointment at first. After my lengthy struggle, I wanted all the attention so I could feel really special.

"Kim tried to make my pregnancy stand out by talking about me first, asking questions, and pointing out how I was doing when people would ask about us. I got over my initial feelings quickly because I knew we had a unique opportunity to share this event as twins. I really loved having her experience and closeness to get through nine months of pregnancy. We looked really cute as pregnant twins and our favorite comment was 'Wow, you two really do everything together!'

"Today we actually have four wonderful boys, two of whom just happen to look alike because they take after their identical mommies.

"As adults we have grown to not be competitive," said Kim. "We have learned from each other and now realize that we are each other's best friend and always have been."

Teamwork

It has become obvious to me that sometimes the twin connection will override a competitive spirit to the point where the twins unconsciously discover that they have great teamwork. Dawn Koenigsberg and Daphne Jordan, age forty, are living proof. Despite being separated for much of their adulthood, they have unknowingly lived their lives in parallel. Today they live in the same city and complement each other in a number of ways. Their teamwork has really paid off for them in their professional lives. Together they run a very successful dating service, called Datewise, in Columbia, South Carolina.

"Our twin bond is very important to us," said Daphne. "We get along so well—especially in business. We actually learned this back when we were nineteen years old and very broke. We would go to a little local hamburger joint where there were pool tables. We couldn't afford to even buy a beer and we realized at an early age, if we played a game of pool, one of us would always play very well and we would always win. We realized that we had this great balance.

"In business today we'll go to a meeting, and we'll be in the car on the way and I'll notice that I forgot this and that. Dawn will say, 'Don't worry about it; I've got it.'" Dawn added, "The next time we go to a meeting, Daphne will be in the same frame of mind and I will say, 'Don't worry, I've got it.' Together we're always prepared because the other one has always got the support materials. We are two minds working as one. Even when we're debating, we quickly figure out we want to get to the same point and the debate ends. Even if we have different ways of doing things, our goals are always the same. It's been a great partnership."

In many cases, competition between twins can be very healthy and provide a number of genuine benefits. Twins can learn from each other as well as take pride in each other's accomplishments. They can help each other to excel, whether it's in school, sports, or the pursuit of a rewarding career. And they can have fun when competing with each other—because in the end, they know their love is real and there for a lifetime.

CHAPTER SIX

The Outside World

While few would argue that no one can be any closer in a relationship than some twin sets, twins cannot live by twins alone. There are many other people who come in and out of relationships with these pairs: families, friends, lovers, and spouses.

Some of these external relationships enhance the lives of these twins; others can cause real harm. It's not uncommon to hear tales of boyfriends, girlfriends, husbands, and wives who just cannot cope with "the twin thing." They might be jealous of the bond or perhaps they just don't understand the importance of this other person.

Others may be ultra supportive because they do understand and respect the tie that binds. I have heard of spouses who lovingly sent their husbands or wives off to Twinsburg, Ohio, for the annual Twins Days Festival. They know how important it is for the twins to celebrate their relationship—and to feel special among others like them.

Dating

The adventure begins with dating. For twins, the dating scene can be described with an abundance of adjectives—fun, horrible, mischievous, annoying, degrading, wonderful, you name it. The experiences are as diverse as the twins themselves.

"The first question that is always asked of a twin, especially a male twin, is 'Did you switch girlfriends?' And any woman who is not smart enough to figure out if they did, and to know there is a difference between the twins, shouldn't be involved with a twin in the first place." So say handsome twin brothers Andrew and Anthony Hill.

The assumption is that all twins play tricks in the romance department. After all, they look, sound, and act the same. It would be so easy to fool somebody, so why not? Part of the answer lies with some twins' life-long struggle to find themselves.

"We really didn't play tricks," said Retha Fielding, fifty. "It was such a struggle just to have an identity. Maybe once Letha and I played a trick on our boyfriends. The truth is once we started dating, our boyfriends didn't know who came to the door. And then they'd ask the other twin out. They thought we were interchangeable. Most people thought we were a set. One person instead of two people. We didn't want that. We didn't want to be a set.

"The only trick that I can remember is the one time my twin played a joke on my boyfriend when I was on the phone. I had to set the phone down for some reason and go somewhere. She picked up the handset and told him she was tired of talking to him and hearing from him. He, of course, thought it was me as we sound identical. It took me awhile to convince him it wasn't me. He certainly couldn't tell."

Marie Queen and Wynona Newberry, now eighty-seven, admit they weren't quite so innocent in the trick department. Marie remembered, "We dated one young man for about three months and he thought there was only one of us. It worked like this. I dated him one time and she dated him the next time. I think we were about eighteen or nineteen. It didn't last too long. When he found out there were two of us, he took off."

For the most part, twins themselves tend to be very honest in their relationships. And when they're not honest, it's in the spirit of playfulness and should not be considered a mean-spirited prank. Sometimes breakups with twins are not even their fault. In the case of Andrew and Anthony, they were victims of mixed-up hearts.

"When we were growing up in high school, Andrew and I were so close that girlfriends were not that important," said Anthony. "If we had a girlfriend, then that was great. If we didn't, it was no problem. We did date a set of girls in high school—we dated them for about three or four months. All of a sudden, they ended it with us for no apparent reason. They said, 'Guys, we just can't do this anymore. We want to break up.' We never understood why. We didn't have a clue.

"A few years after we graduated from high school, I came into contact with one of them at my younger brother's college. I told her that Andrew and I had always been perplexed as to why she and the other girl broke up with us so suddenly. It was just wham! We're broken up. She said that she and the other girl tried and tried to figure out a way of switching us around. After a period of time, they had both figured out that they liked the wrong twin. They were dating the wrong brothers! They figured that they had already settled into the relationship, so they dumped us."

Jackie Gagnon and Jeannine St. Hilaire remember the times when they would compete with each other for the same guy. Typically Jackie would date the person first. She said, "They always began dating me and then they would go to my twin second. They were attracted to us both. She would always be their favorite, though. I was the one always left behind. Jeannine would always win out." In the end, both Jackie and Jeannine married men who did not date the both of them.

Does being an identical twin make it any easier to attract the opposite sex? Some twins say yes. When you see not one but two attractive people who look exactly the same, it's hard not to be interested. The only drawback is that many twins would rather not be liked for novelty sake alone. Such are the feelings of Jon and Chris Scamahorne, who are two attractive nineteen year-olds. "Some girls say they like me because I'm cute, but I would rather they like me for my personality," said Jon. "And some people say I wouldn't be so popular if I weren't a twin. I can't help that I'm a twin. I want people to be my friend because of my personality—not because I'm a twin."

"Girlfriends like us for our personalities," said Chris. "Some like me and not him; and vice versa. Some girls have their own opinions. They think I'm cuter or they think he's cuter. Some say they would never date my brother because of how he is. Those are the young women who really get to know us."

Jon added, "About the only trick we play is that sometimes when we go out with a girl we may ask her what she thinks of 'my brother,' and then we tell her who we really are."

The Third Wheel

While the tricks are minor and playful, dating tends to get more serious when the relationship with the twin is introduced. Many girlfriends and boyfriends have a hard time with the twins' closeness or bond. For the twins, there is a critical need for the new partner to understand the role of the brother or sister. Some boyfriends and girlfriends just don't get it.

"They feel they come second," said sisters Tara Behnke and Christine Rizzo, age thirty. "And they are not too happy about it. The truth is sometimes they do come second. We probably will never have a relationship with someone else like we have with each other. Sometimes we go out together and then come home and sit on the bed and talk until three in the morning about what happened that night. Our boyfriends could never understand what we had to talk about to each other. They just didn't understand."

"Hopefully we will find a set of twins and marry them," said twenty-three-year-old Mike and Chuck Szopo. "We're best friends. We live together now. Why get two houses when it's cheaper to live together?"

When asked if they would like to go through life together, the answer came in stereo: "Yes, we think that's the way it's going to go."

Linda and Lisa Lieske, thirty-one, have similar feelings about staying together. Their emphasis, however, is on spouses acknowledging and respecting their twin relationship. "We want to get married and have kids. We really don't want to find twin boys, but she has to like whom I marry and I have to like whom she marries. They have to go through a judging process. If they didn't understand our relationship, then they would simply have to live with it."

Linda says she had one boyfriend that was jealous because she spent so much time with her family. Lisa added, "It's hard for one of us to have a boyfriend and not the other, because you always feel that the other is uncomfortable. And this is just how we feel; we're not saying it's this way for every twin. The truth is we both have to like each other's boyfriend. We are very protective of each other. We want what's best for the other—and we know what's best."

Lisa continued, "You don't hold back with your opinions. You say, 'I don't like that person.' Maybe a friend wouldn't tell you right away, but we have no trouble telling each other what we think. There is 100 percent honesty there."

They both agree that it's an almost "you marry me, you marry my sister" type of situation. They reiterated that the husband, boyfriend, or partner would have to respect the relationship they have.

The Wedding

Weddings can be one of the most joyous events in a lifetime. Some twins, like Craig and Mark Sanders, thirty-five-year-old identical creators of the Web site Twinstuff.com, found identical blushing brides, and married them in a double ceremony.[14] The boy twins met the girl twins at the annual Twins Days Festival in Twinsburg, Ohio. Today the couples live next door to one another.

Jeanne Corfee and Eleanor (Ellie) Killebrew Brown, who were known in their youth as the All-American Toni Twins, also opted for a double wedding although they didn't marry matching brothers. Ellie's boyfriend (and later fiancé) introduced her twin, Jeanne, to a wonderful young man named Fred Corfee. When the time came for the twins to get married, there was no question that they would share the special day. Because the young women were international celebrities, several local newspapers documented their pre-wedding activities. They were photographed selecting their china, crystal, and silver, as well as their wedding gowns. It came as no surprise that they picked many of the same patterns. They also selected the same wedding dress.

On the arms of their beaming father, and in front of five hundred of their closest friends, the Toni Twins were married.

"It was wonderful because if one of us had gotten married and the other hadn't, one of us would have been very sad and would have been left alone," said Jeanne. "This way, we both had our husbands when we went away and lived in different cities, and everything was fine. We weren't upset or unhappy with the separation at all because we had them. The double wedding was lovely. I have to mention that we received identical presents. Everyone bought two."

Double twin weddings are somewhat rare. What is not so unique is the surprise one family gets when they find out the bride- or groom-to-be has a mirror image. Such was the case with Pat Halpin, forty-four, and his brother, Mike.

Pat talked about both weddings: "He was the best man in my wedding and I was the best man in his. I remember having to give a toast—only this toast wasn't completely focused on my beautiful bride. The toast was that I had to introduce Mike to all the people on the bride's side because most had never met him. Some barely knew he existed. Imagine their surprise when two of us stood at the altar. I went on to tell some nice stories about when we were growing up. It was fun."

It's important to many twins that their day is special and that it belongs only to them and their betrothed. It's not to say that the twin won't be an integral part of the ceremony, but for some, this event is not to be intimately shared. Jenny and Penny Waggoner, twenty-seven, are adamant about this. "We want our wedding days to be separate." Both concede, however, that they will be in each other's weddings, not far from each other's side.

Marry Me, Marry My Twin

"I now pronounce you husband and wife—and twin." To some it's an agreeable combination that causes all three to rejoice. To others, it can be a catalyst for misunderstandings, hurt feelings, and general unhappiness. It can also be a cause for separation and divorce. You have to wonder why this threesome is good for some and disastrous for others. Twins tell us it all depends on the attitude of the spouse entering the relationship.

Judy Fischer, thirty-seven, explained. "It's like her ex-husband tried to split us up. He didn't want me to see my twin or even talk to her. We had to find a way to see each other, and to this day he still has a problem with it." Sister Beth Whitaker agreed and said. "He was very jealous of the relationship. Yes, he tried to split us up. Now he's gone!"

Dawn Jordan's husband was just the opposite. "He came from a challenging family environment as I did, and he just knew that I was a package deal. He accepted from the very beginning that I was a part of a very close twosome. If he wanted to be jealous of Daphne, then he would lose me. There was no one that would keep me from Daphne. And he always knew that if I needed to be there, he would either support me and go with me or just say, 'You go, and I'll be fine.'"

Twin sister Daphne Koenigsberg had an opposite experience. She said, "I have always gone through jealous partners, maybe because they see Dawn as a threat to me. They always think that Dawn can talk me into doing something or can manipulate my mind but she can't. People have a tendency to believe that I'm not as independent as I am."

Dawn added, "I guess that comes from our person-alities because I'm so boisterous and up front with my feelings where as Daphne doesn't tend to speak out as much. It's not that she comes across as being more passive, but maybe a little more reserved. I guess it's our presentation. Daphne's husband was extremely jealous of me."

Jealousy, not enough attention, lack of confidence. It's hard to pinpoint why some spouses never quite accept that twins are generally rooted in each other. Heather Reser, twenty-nine, knows all too well how that can happen. She said, "My husband doesn't understand the twin thing and he thinks its weird. He feels threatened by it."

"He doesn't know me very well," added twin Leslie. "And it's been a little difficult getting to know him over the years because of his work and projects around the house. In the past, we've heard him say, 'You guys are in your own world when you're together.' It's true! Then to his credit, he steps back and just lets us do our thing. He's never come to Twinsburg because he knows it's our weekend. He may not like it, but he knows that it's something that we have to do and that we've been doing it since we were six. It's not like he didn't know we were twins when he and Heather got married. He had to have known that there would be this very special bond between Heather and I."

Betty Burton and Bert Polley, seventy, reminisce about the husband days. Bert moved in with Betty when her husband died. "When she moved in with me and my husband, the children said maybe it would cause trouble," said Betty. "But my husband said it wouldn't. Sometimes he was better to her than he was to me." Bert agreed, "Yes, he was." Then Betty added— with a twinkle in her eye, "Like many husbands of a twin, he liked to tell people that he had two wives."

Both Betty's and Bert's husbands have since passed on. In retrospect, the women say their husbands always made sure they got together a lot. They knew the twins had a bond and would tell each other things they would tell no others. The sisters say they were good husbands.

Fred Corfee has also been a good husband to his wife, Jeanne, and a good brother-in-law to her twin, Ellie. For a period of about seventeen years when Ellie was a widow, Fred used to take great pleasure in escorting the two identical beauties everywhere. One day a woman on the street came up to the group and said, "Oh, you must be twins!" Fred retorted, "No, we're triplets." The woman shot right back at him and said, "Then you must be the ugly one!"

Ed and Don MaKielski, seventy-two, have each been married for forty-eight years. Ed had been going out with a young woman and actually picked out her roommate as a blind date for his brother. Don and the roommate ended up getting married. They admitted, though, that the relationship with each other was much different from the relationship with their wives.

"In some ways we are closer to each other than to our wives," Ed said. "We have certain ways of confiding in each other. We can talk about things to each other that we cannot talk about even to our wives."

Twins like Mary and Ella believe the old saying that you don't just marry the bride, you marry the family. "My husband always says he has two wives," said Mary McAraw DiAngelo, sixty-nine. "He likes that." In this case, you also marry the twin. So the question becomes, do twins have to approve of each other's choice for matrimony? Ella has the answer. "No, but it would help if you liked them!"

There's no doubt that being the spouse of a twin can have its ups and downs. The ups can be rich and full of great fun. But the downs can provide twinges of confusion and doubt. Le Melcher talked about the special ladies in his life: "Soon after my brother, Pete, was married—he got married a year or so before I did—his wife, thinking I was Pete, grabbed me from behind at a cocktail party. The woman I was dating, who is now my wife, said, 'That woman is a bimbo; I would never make that mistake.' A week later, my wife grabbed Pete from behind at a party. On both occasions we were wearing different clothes. Both of our wives swear there is nothing identical about us—they say they can tell us apart in a heartbeat. Yet each woman grabbed the wrong one!"

Linda Houk and Laura Fryman, forty-two, say that tale sounds very familiar. Linda recalled, "One time we were having a great day, playing at the golf tournament when my husband pinched Laura's bottom. He said, 'I thought you were Linda!' I said, 'Sure you did!' He said, 'Well, then I guess I owe you one.'"

Twin Envy

Because of the tremendous connection between most twins, a pair will occasionally encounter jealousy from family and friends. It's not that they mean to be envious or jealous. It's just that the twin phenomenon may be uncommon and unfamiliar in some families. It may even be considered somewhat rare in schools or play environments. As a result, people may show some negativity without meaning to. In families in which there are more children than just the twins, siblings might feel slighted in some way. Twins generally attract a lot of attention, whether they want it or not. As a result, there may be some hostility or misunderstanding.

"They are jealous of the closeness," said Jackie Gagnon of her siblings. "There were seven kids in our family and we were spoiled the most. We were always referred to as 'the twins.'"

Kim Smith and Cheryl Bobelak, forty-three, say initially their baby brother had a hard time dealing with their twinness. He was two years younger than them. "He felt like we always got the attention—because we were twins," said Kim. "Once in a while when we would fight we would form a bond with our brother and then we would reverse. Sometimes we would both gang up on him so he could never win." They laugh about it now, and say he does too. They say today, as an adult, he teases them unmercifully and actually loves the fact that they're twins.

The same holds true for Jeannie Van Horn and Joan Pahls Notch, forty. They both have children now. "Our kids just love each other, and both of us too," said Jeannie. "What is interesting is that I think our older siblings are a little jealous. The same holds true for a few friends."

Joan added, "They'll come out and say, 'I wish I had a twin to share my secrets and deepest thoughts. There are things I wouldn't tell my other brothers and sisters or even my parents.'"

Chris Scamahorne, nineteen, has seen the same

reaction from friends only more intense. "Sometimes they get jealous of our bond. Still, they like to hang out with both of us. The bad thing is that sometimes they talk behind Jon's back, or my back. They ask us why each other acts the way we do, and vice versa."

No matter what the behavior of family or friends, most twins take extreme pride in the fact that they are a twin, and they let nothing stop them from telling the world.

"Most of my friends know that I identify myself as a twin," said Andrew Hill, thirty-five. "I'm not happy talking in a crowd without Anthony around, unless I tell them, 'By the way, did you know that I am an identical twin? There's one just like me.' I want them to understand that I don't just have a brother, I have twin brother!"

Andrew added, "Friends ask me why I always have to tell people that I'm a twin. They say, 'Do you always have to say twin?' And I say yes, because there is a difference between having a brother and having a twin brother."

Anthony then said, "I've had friends that have tended to get irritated about me talking too much about being a twin, and I don't really care about what they think. I enjoy talking about it and being one, and if Andrew's not with me, it's a good way for me to remember him."

Do we, singletons, really comprehend the deep, loving relationship most twins have with each other? For the most part, I would say yes. Still, there are some families, friends, lovers, and spouses that may not. When a bond is that strong between two people, the outside world needs to not only recognize it, but also respect and nurture it. And for those who are just beginning to get to know a twin—either in a friendship, dating, or family situation—they need to go into the relationship with an open mind and an accepting heart. Only then, will the relationship offer a win-win outcome.

CHAPTER SEVEN

The Inexplicable

The twin connection has been a source of great mystery throughout the ages. The connection seems to produce unique stories that border on the uncanny or the supernatural.

Having said that, I must also say that twins will be the first to acknowledge that husbands and wives, siblings, and even roommates may have similar abilities. They acknowledge that these pairs of people can often guess what each other is thinking or can read each other's minds. It happens when two people, no matter who they are, spend a lot of time together in close proximity. I'm sure most everyone has been able to answer another person's question before hearing the words—it's a common occurrence among many. But the twin connection goes much farther than that. How do twins know what is happening to the other physically and psychologically? The true answer lies in the twins themselves.

"I am aware of her all of the time," said Connie Wyckoff, of her twin who now lives in another state.

"Two or three years ago I got a call from the hospital telling me that my sister had developed a life-threatening anemia and was hemorrhaging everywhere. I was told she wouldn't make it until I got there. I told them to keep her alive and that they could have my blood for a direct transfusion. On the way down Pete, my husband, kept asking me how she was doing. And I was aware that she was still alive and that she would survive.

"Another time when we were in our twenties," Connie continued, "I felt so physically bad I was sure I had appendicitis and I actually went to the hospital. The doctor said I was having pains similar to labor pains, but that there was nothing medically wrong with me. I later found out my twin was having her baby at that exact time."

"I will know if my twin passes away. I'm sure it must be mental," Connie added. "I can almost feel her in my mind. I can call her and she can tell me what color clothes I'm wearing. I'm a pretty good sender and she's a pretty good receiver. We have a lot of ESP between the two of us. Even with all of this closeness, we are not friends and find it hard to be together for any length of time. I still love her very much and wish we had the loving close relationship of most twins."

Bob Lawrence is a sixty-four-year-old identical twin who has a similar connection to his twin Bill.

"There is a physical closeness. You hear that twins feel each other's pain, but it's not true for us. However, there is a physical connection. One time Bill was in the hospital and had to have a catheter removed. I was twelve miles away. Within an hour of the catheter being removed, I experienced bleeding that was very similar to Bill's."

Andrew and Anthony Hill have experienced what they call blood dreams. Like Bill and Bob, they have bled for no apparent reason other than what must be a physical connection to their twin. Their story is remarkable. Anthony said, "I worked as a lifeguard in high school. Andrew worked at a pizza place. It was pretty common for me to come in at the end of the day and go to bed, but my brother would have to work until midnight or so. One night, he ended the evening by cutting his finger on his left hand. He's left-handed; I'm right-handed. We are mirror twins. Anyway, he came in and went to bed. The next morning, I woke up and my right hand is split in the same spot where his finger has been cut. Unbelievable to some, but to us, it just happens."

"My twin, Judy, got into a really bad accident with a truck, a semi. I knew something was terribly wrong," said Beth Whitaker. "I didn't know what it was; it was just a feeling that something was not right.

We got a phone call about a half-hour later from the state highway patrol saying she had been in an accident. But it's more just a feeling that something is not right. It is a sick feeling in the bottom of your stomach. It just doesn't go away until you find out what the cause of it is. You know it involves your twin."

Cheryl Smith and Kim Bobelak have similar stories. "Where do we begin?" said Cheryl. "When Kim was in Chicago I happened to call her. I had had a pain in my left arm and she had had a pain in her left arm. A few days—or maybe it was even weeks later—we talked about it. A bee had stung her and I had felt the same sensation."

Physical warning signs are not uncommon among twins. In fact, 50 percent of the twins I talked to reported these types of stories. The severity varies—an ache here; a pain there. They are red flag alerts that appear out of nowhere but persevere. Sometimes they go away and the twin experiences a sense of overwhelming relief only to find out later that his or her sibling went through either an emotionally or physically traumatic situation. Other times, the nagging feeling won't disappear until the twin takes action—either by calling or physically going to see the other. Whatever the case may be, many twins are supercognizant of the other's physical and emotional well-being.

Take the case of Jeannine St. Hilaire and Jackie Gagnon, for example. Jackie was in labor with her son and her twin was at work. Out of the blue, Jeannine became ill for no reason. Later the pair figured out that it must have been some telepathic communication that had physical properties as well. To this day, they find it hard to explain.

Cheryl Smith also had a very strong feeling about her twin's pregnancy. "I knew when Kim had her first child. I called her on the phone and said, 'I'm an aunt, aren't I?' I just had this strange overwhelming feeling that something important was happening to her.

The Coincidence Factor

The everyday stories may not be as dramatic, but they certainly validate that there is a strange and wonderful connection between twins—something that few of us singletons have ever known. Take the wardrobe stories. You might think that two people who have grown up and shared the same experiences throughout their childhood and adolescent years might have similar tastes in clothing. But the events that take place as grownups are hard to explain away.

Laura Houk and Linda Fryman make an annual pilgrimage to Twinsburg, Ohio, for the Twins Days

Festival. They, like the three thousand other sets of twins, like to take advantage of the festival to dress alike. So they plan and plan for this special occasion. Laura lives in Ohio and Linda lives in Arizona. "For this trip, I had ordered some sunglasses out of *Golf Magazine for Women.* I bought her a pair because we wanted to wear the same thing. When I got here, I found out that she already had the same pair," Laura reported.

Linda says there is more. "We always have a fit about whether our hair is going to look alike. But the truth is, we always look alike—no matter what. For this trip, we didn't know if we would match. We did! If you look at us, you'll see that our hair matches exactly. We had no way of knowing."

For most female twins, there is usually a dress story. Marie and Wynona tell theirs. "Marie was in Boston and I was in Jacksonville, Florida," said Wynona. "Marie bought a new dress and when we chatted she said she would have bought me one if there had been two. She had no idea that I had actually bought the same dress that day."

Ella McAraw and Mary McAraw DiAngelo had a similar story. Ella said, "Often we buy clothes and we are not together. Later we find out they are exactly the same outfits from the same major department stores. It really happens a lot."

Then there's Joan Pahls Notch who lives twenty minutes from her twin. She tells the story of her sister's similarity in style. "Jeannie came over to do my lawn. Oddly enough, we both had our hair pulled up in ponytails and had red shirts on. We didn't know we were going to do that—it just happened. We still do things like unknowingly dressing the same even though we live a fair distance away."

Marie Queen, eighty-seven, talks about how her sister, Wynona, lost a tooth, and then a few weeks later, she lost the same tooth. You might wonder about a genetic predisposition for tooth loss, or perhaps similar brushing techniques and dental care. But the same tooth?

A similar thing happened to my twins. Max had a loose tooth in the front—it was his first and we thought he might lose it any day. Sam, on the other hand, didn't have any loose teeth. One day the boys came home from school, and Sam reported that he had lost a tooth. My husband and I did a double take. We were very surprised. Sam's tooth wasn't even wiggly. We were even more surprised to see that the tooth he lost was the same as Max's wiggly tooth but on the opposite side. The fact that Sam and Max are mirrored twins may explain it. Of course, within thirty minutes Max lost his.

Christine Grimm and her sister, Angelika, live an ocean apart. Angelika still lives in Germany where they were born. Christine moved to the United States about ten years ago. Christine said, "When we get together, we notice little things—especially when we cook together. Even though we have lived apart for nearly a decade, we both have a fascination with Italian and Thai food. And we've discovered that we are so much alike in the way we cook and the way we prepare food. For example, instead of washing our mushrooms, we actually peel them. (We both peel them to get better flavor.) When I first saw her do it, I said 'I do that!' It's little coincidences like that that still surprise us today."

Jenna and Jessi Clayton talk about their medicine incident. Jessi said, "I remember the time I had to take a certain type of medicine. I immediately got a rash. Later it turned out that Jenna had to take the same kind of medicine. She didn't get a rash—but I did and headaches. I got Jenna's rash when *she* was taking the medicine. Sometimes you just can't win."

Keith Hogan said, "I can remember one time Kevin got a whooping. I wasn't with him but for some strange reason I started crying because I knew he had just had a whooping. We were between ten and twelve years old then. I just started crying and when I got home I said, 'What did you do?'"

Mike and Chuck Szopo have that same connection. Chuck said, "When I got my first ticket my whole spine kind of went numb. And my brother, Mike, who was nowhere in site, said he had felt it. We both can feel when really bad things are going to happen—not good things, only bad."

Donna DeLozier's connection stories run the gamut from shopping to shared pain. "There are so many incidents where we have inexplicably done the same thing or felt the same way," Donna said. "Although we live apart, Dianne and I used to send our mother the same birthday card—and, of course, laugh about it when we found out. We usually send each other gifts for holidays, but this past Valentine's Day we didn't because Dianne was coming to visit a couple of weeks later. I'm an arts and crafts person so I had made her a heart basket. I had lined it and filled it with potpourri. When we exchanged gifts I started laughing because her gift to me was a heart basket just a little bit smaller. She smiled and said, 'I guess I know what I'm getting.'"

Donna continued, "I remember a more serious event in our lives in which our connection became very apparent. My mother had called to wish me a happy birthday. A little while later I got a second call from my mother again to tell me that Dianne had fallen and shattered her arm—but they didn't tell me which arm. They admitted her to the hospital. The odd thing was that my arm had been hurting all day. After my mother's call, I called Dianne and she admitted that she had shattered her arm. I asked her, 'Would you please take something for pain?'"

Exact gifts, birthday cards, clothing, and even cooking styles seem to pop up more than you'd expect when talking to twins about their shared experiences. I have yet to find a set of twins in my research that has not had at least one of these experiences. They are fun to talk about. Maybe some of the events are coincidental, but they play an important role in describing the relationship between these two special people.

Heather Reser and Leslie Rapp live miles apart—one twin in Ohio, the other in Indiana—yet they still have a lot of things in common. "We still say the same things at the same time; we don't practice it," said Leslie. "We'll buy the same birthday cards for my mom even though we're in different states. I think we sense things. If we haven't talked to each other in awhile, we'll go to call each other about the same time. With us, there's a real timing thing."

The "birthday card experience" is a common story among twins, and it surfaces again and again. Renee

Richardson and Rhonda Kulpinski are no exception to this experience. They, too, live far away from each other. "Now that we live so far apart, there are things that we've done that are odd," said Renee. "We might cook the exact same thing one night or send each other the same birthday card even though we live over six hundred miles apart. In the case of the birthday card, we even sent them on the same day. I thought mine came back to me, and she thought the same thing. Things like that really surprise us because we've lived separately now for fourteen years and it was only four years ago that we became close again. For ten years before that, we weren't close emotionally."

The Same Strokes

The coincidences are astonishing. Even in academics, they are plentiful. From the moment my husband and I learned that we were to have twins, we made the decision to help them cherish their brotherhood yet become individuals. We first separated them academically in preschool. Sam had his class, his teacher, and friends, and Max had his. They really enjoyed their freedom from each other during class time, but found themselves gravitating to each other on the playground. For them, it was a good mix. When they hit kindergarten after two years of preschool, they were old-timers at being alone in the world of education. Separation was no big deal to them. They liked it.

The surprising thing to us was that when report card time came around in kindergarten, they couldn't have been matched more perfectly. During our parent-teacher conference for Max, we were told that he knew all of his letters except for P, Q, and R, he could count up to thirty-nine, and he was a bit of a talker—very social. Then it was Sam's turn. His teacher said he knew all of his letters except—surprise—P, Q, and R, and he could count up to thirty-nine. And he was a talker—very social. How could this be? They had been separated academically for nearly three years with different teachers, different teaching styles, and different classroom environments.

It was the same story for Kim Smith and Cheryl Bobelak. Kim reported, "In Latin class we had a project where we had to draw maps. We did them apart and the teacher was dumbfounded because when he compared them we had used the same colors to color each area. We even used the same strokes."

Right Time, Right Place

Owen Murphy is a twenty-four-year-old fraternal twin who looks identical to his brother, Adam. Owen remembered, "There have been three different occasions I can remember that my brother was coming in from a distance to meet me at a bar, or at a club. The first two times, we ended up hopping in line at the exact same time after having come in separately from two different locations.

"The third time I was with another person. Adam was in a different car coming in from a location two hours away. I got to an intersection and the car that I went to wave on at the stop sign was my brother who was also looking for a parking space. Coming from two hours away and arriving at the exact location at the exact same time, was that a coincidence? I don't know."

Stephanie Winger and Jennifer Wilcox are fraternal twins and wonder about their connection. "I think it's more like she's my sister and we happen to be the same age so I'm probably closer to her than my other two sisters," Stephanie said. "But when we were together, we would go through the same things at the same time. With things like playing Pictionary, we could read each other's minds somewhat. I don't know whether it was because we were around each other so much or what."

Dreams

It's hard to imagine two people being so connected that they share each other's thoughts. It's harder still to imagine them sharing one another's pain. But it's even more mind-boggling to fathom two people sharing each other's dreams. When I talk to twins about their dreams, I believe them. They are honest and genuine when they tell these stories. By recalling the dreams, twins put themselves into a very vulnerable position. The dreams are personal, and many times it's clear that they themselves continue to be perplexed about how and why these dreams occur.

Paul Golde recalls a dream long ago: "There was one really interesting head shaker that was just so weird. My twin Rick and I were about twelve years old and I still remember that Saturday morning. We always had breakfast and dinner as a family. This one Saturday morning, I came stumbling to the breakfast table. I had had a really bad dream; it was so frightening and seemed so real. It really affected me. I sat down and started telling everyone about it. We were

walking through this primeval forest. Giant ptero-
dactyls scooped Rick and me up; we were screaming.
I could see Rick in the jaws of the pterodactyl. Then I
looked over at Rick at the breakfast table and he had
a pale look on his face. He had had that same dream
a couple of nights ago and didn't tell anybody. We all
still remember that morning."

"I recently had a pretty bizarre twin dream," said
Sarah Caton, age twenty-five. "My twin, Claire, started
getting very serious with her boyfriend last spring.
One night this past summer I dreamed that she
decided to get married. It was such a vivid dream that
it was all I could think about the next morning. I was
even scripting my toast to her for her rehearsal dinner
on my drive downtown to work. Then around ten that
morning I called her to tell her about my dream. After
I told her the story, she proceeded to tell me that she
and her boyfriend had decided the night before to get
engaged by the end of the year."

Claire recounts a different type of dream experience—one in which the twin twenty-five-year-olds
shared the exact dream on the same night: "On this
particular night I fell asleep in my older sister's bed
and Sarah fell asleep in my mom's bed downstairs.
When my older sister, Carrie, got home, I woke up to
find her standing over me and laughing. She told me

that I was dreaming, but I was actually in that state between sleep and consciousness. I was frantically looking for the 'papers' that I needed. While I was laughing with her, I still knew the importance of finding those papers. When Mom woke Sarah up that same night, she had been having the exact same dream, and *they* encountered exactly the same experience with the 'papers.'"

Both identical dreams and dreams that present clues to the future are prevalent among twins. The premonition dreams seem to come true in many cases. Le Melcher recalls hearing about a dream his twin had about him: "There was a time I was in Europe and my twin brother, Pete, was in the States. I was in a bad car accident. My mother later told me that Pete had a dream that I was hit by a car two days before the accident. Maybe a month or two later, I talked to Pete about the incident and he confirmed that he had talked to our mother about the dream."

Christine Grimm said, "When I moved to New York from Germany about nine years ago, I stayed in New York for three months just to see if I'd like it or not. I hadn't planned on actually going back to Germany for good after that, but I decided I needed some more time in my hometown in Germany to tie up loose ends and get a perspective of my future in New York. I hadn't told anyone in Germany that I would be coming home or that I had booked a flight that day. The next morning, the phone woke me up. It was my twin, Angelika, in Germany. She was crying because she had a dream in which I was coming home. She was crying because upon waking up, she had realized it was only a dream. To her surprise, I told her it wasn't a dream, and that I had actually booked my flight around the same time she slept in Germany. As you can imagine, the tears turned into big smiles."

There are few twins, especially identical twins, who don't have stories such as these. Some may brush off the stories as normal, everyday events—others may acquiesce that they are special and yes, a little unusual. Many twins rejoice in their ability to know and feel and experience each other's lives. Again, it is a special gift—one that validates their emotional and spiritual connections time and time again.

CHAPTER EIGHT

The Void

The loss of a loved one is one of the hardest life experiences we all must go through. The emotions we experience are diverse—pain, anger, depression, and denial. I am fortunate that it wasn't until I was in my late twenties that I was forced to go through the process. It was very difficult. My grief over the death of my grandfather was both intense and deep. Before losing him, I couldn't understand or relate to the pain caused by death. I believe it is the same way with twin loss.

Several of the twins I talked to know the grief all too well. When they lost their twin, the grief was just as intense as it might be after losing a child—only different. The depth of their emotions over the loss of their twin is often beyond comprehension to those of us who are only children or who have traditional brothers and sisters. Many times, just as their grief runs deep so does their silence. Twins who have lost twins often retreat into themselves because the world won't—and can't—understand.

In general, there are many myths about grief. One myth is that all losses are the same. Another is that all people grieve in the same way and grief gradually decreases over time. One of the biggest myths about bereavement is that you will bounce back to your regular self and be the same after the death as you were before your loved one died. These myths often cause more pain for the person who is grieving.

Grieving is a very personal experience, and every person handles the process differently. Twinless twins are no exception. Whether they have lost their twin to illness, sudden death, murder, or suicide, the pain can consume them. Twinless twins have some of the toughest obstacles to overcome. For identical twins, they are reminded of their partner in life every time they look in the mirror. Friends and family mistake them for the one who has passed. There are painful reminders every day of their lives, and the grieving continues.

Unimaginable Loss

"People just don't understand what you go through when you lose a twin," said Thelma Ellis. "They try to be helpful by sharing their stories about losing a parent, sibling, or child, but it isn't the same. You really can't compare it. It is just part of you. You keep looking around to see your twin, but she's not there.

She was a part of me that I want to reach out and bring back. I want her to still be here, and I know she won't."

Thelma and her twin, Velma, were extremely close. When they were born, they weighed a mere three and a half and three pounds respectively. Their daddy nicknamed them "Heavy" and "Pee Wee." They weren't identical, but Thelma says they had a real closeness physically, emotionally, and spiritually. They looked and sounded alike.

"When we were little, we had to pick cotton and I was always so scared of the worms. Velma would always come back and check to make sure the worms were on the leaves and not on me. She would always help me out. When she was finished picking her cotton, she would help me finish my row so I wouldn't get into trouble. We always helped each other out that way."

At age forty-six, Thelma lost her twin after a lengthy illness. Velma had actually kept her illness hidden from her twin for nearly seven years.

"When I asked her why she didn't tell me, she said she didn't want to hurt me. We hugged and hugged each other, and from that time on, we spent a lot of time together, just talking about her hurt and her pain. I loved her so much.

"After the funeral, I came back to my home and got to the point where I didn't want to get out of bed. If I combed my hair, I would see her in the mirror. If I talked to people, I would hear her voice. I couldn't do anything except to stay real still. I didn't want to do anything to remind me of her—everything reminded me of her."

Thirty-six-year-old Tom Carlock lost his twin, Tim, two years ago. They were identical in every way except for the birthmark behind Tom's ear. They were about as close as twins can be.

"Growing up, we shared everything and were never apart," Tom said. "I remember our mom telling us that as babies, she couldn't separate us or we would both start to cry. We knew each other better than anyone. After all, we were two halves of a whole. We were constantly finishing each other's sentences, pulling pranks on others, and switching classes. Our lives were filled with a special bond that only twins can experience.

"Somehow I knew that I was going to lose Tim about six weeks before he found out he was infected with HIV. Something deep within me told me that the most wonderful gift in my life was about to be taken from me. 'I die, Horatio' were his words to me as he quoted Shakespeare after hearing the diagnosis. His eyes seemed to echo my lament when he told me."

Tim only lived about three and a half years with HIV before it ravaged his body. Tom took care of him the last year of his life. He also ensured that Tim had as many happy moments as he could before he became housebound. When Tim died, Tom used travel to try to heal his wounds.

"After Tim died, I felt so naked. Half of me had died and it was like trying to be born again as one. I couldn't seem to do it. I didn't want to do it. I thought of suicide many times after Tim died, but my promise to him—to be 'all right'—kept me from it. 'I will be all right,' I kept saying to myself—for Tim. I can understand why the rate of suicide among twinless twins is so high. Never in my life have I felt so lost."

Mary Hartung Wetter, forty-four, feels lost too. It has been two years since she lost her identical twin sister, Margaret Hartung. Margaret had suffered from cancer for the majority of her adult life. Her pain began at age twenty-eight with uterine cancer, which eventually progressed to her colon, lungs, and then brain. Throughout her battle with cancer, she remained strong and positive because of her children and her twin.

"They say one twin is always the meek and mild one while the other one is tough and strong," said

Mary. "I used to think that I was the stronger twin because I raised two children on my own and worked two jobs to provide for them. When I think about it now, I wasn't the strong one. She lived and never let the cancer get her down. I wasn't the strong one.

"We were so close that losing her has destroyed my life in a major way. I used to be happy and carefree and wouldn't let much bother me. Now I feel like I've lost all of that—I've lost everything. I had to quit my job because she had worked there too. People would see me and tell me how they were thinking about her. There is only so much you can handle. I don't celebrate my birthday anymore. What's the point? All through the years we always celebrated our birthday together. There is no reason to celebrate now."

When a person loses a twin, the darkness seems to stretch on endlessly. As Thelma, Tom, and Mary have said, the reminders are everywhere—in the mirror, in their own voices, and in the good wishes of coworkers. For singletons, it's hard to imagine the pain twinless twins have when they see their own reflection. Throughout the course of a lifetime, the twins' identities have been enveloped in each other. They have been confidants, advisers, and soul mates.

Joyce Durren, sixty-five, lost her twin, Joanne, to cancer very quickly. They had little time together in the end. "I remember her saying to me, 'I hate this worse for you than I do for myself.' I knew she meant it. Watching her suffer was horrendous. When she was in such pain, I asked her to let me have the pain so she could get some rest. I would have suffered it for her if I only could.

"Even though we didn't agree on everything, which would have been impossible even for twins, she loved me as much as I loved her. And we respected each other's differences. I cherish that. We accepted each other just the way we were.

"I allow myself feelings of anger and sadness, but I can't stay with them very long. Grieving is very tiring and Joanne's death has left me so empty."

Gail Rubinfeld, forty-eight, writes, "I must say it's rather bizarre to be even sitting here writing to you about the loss of my identical twin sister, Marian. It is two years now since she died and it seems like just two months. We used to e-mail each other every day, and for a moment, it's hard to believe she is really gone."

Gail lost her sister to breast cancer. "No one knew how sick she was; she was so brave and strong. To lose Miri, that was her nickname, is like losing a part of myself—my youth, my innocence, my future.

"Most days are the same. You go about your life without someone you love very much. Birthdays are the worst. I once wanted my 'own day' and now I wish I could share our birthdays with her forever. We expected to walk along the beach together as old ladies after our husbands were gone. We always planned to have each other. I never in my wildest days thought I would lose Miri."

The loss is devastating. The pain—even worse. And there's more. With Gail, there is also fear. Because she is an identical twin to Miri, it's possible that she, too, might have the genetic predisposition for cancer.

"Miri died because of the improper care she received," she explained. "Her doctors dismissed her symptoms. I told her to go for a second opinion. Then I got the call. 'Gail, I have breast cancer. Can you call Mommy and Daddy and tell them? I can't.' It's hard to explain the loss of this brave, beautiful, caring woman. I go every six months for checkups," said Gail. "I am scared that I am next."

A Life Stolen

The sudden death of a loved one leaves questions that may never be answered. Why did it have to happen? Why to her and not to me? How can someone so good be taken at such a young age? Even if you can find the answers, they may not really help ease the pain. In the case of twins, where the connection is so strong, the puzzlement can go on for a lifetime. So can the "what ifs?"

Michele Turner, fifty-eight, and her identical twin, Michon, had a wonderful childhood. They were born and reared near Reno, Nevada. When they were eighteen, they were the Olympic Queens for the 1960 Winter Olympics in Squaw Valley, California. They were beautiful, friendly, and extremely close. They loved to dress alike, and planned to cherish their lives together.

"The first time we were separated was when Michon got married and moved away," said Michele. "When she was living in New Mexico, we could only communicate by writing letters. She didn't have a phone. It was hard. I can say that we truly lived to be with each other. We always talked about someday going to the old folk's home together. It was the most wonderful feeling in the world to be a twin with her.

"In 1971, I remember having a terrible feeling as I was getting ready to travel to New Mexico to see her. I said to my husband that something had happened to my sister and I didn't know what it was. I just knew something had happened. Then I got a call from my mother. There had been a plane crash. Michon, her husband, and their six-year-old daughter, Tori, had been circling over their ranch looking for a coyote that had killed their sheep. All three were killed. We found out about six hours later that their son had been on the ground with the riders and was still alive.

"It's been thirty years, but it is still so lonely without her. I still think about her every minute. I feel like only half of me is here. But I made up my mind that I would be okay and that her son would do well. We had promised each other that we would take care of each other's children if something were to happen. He is like my son. He named his first daughter after my sister.

"I thank God every day that I am a twin and that I had her for as long as I did. She continues to be with me every minute."

Peter Kroneman, twenty-six, lost his twin on May 10, 2000. The wounds are fresh and they are deep. "My brother, Eric, was on his way home from work. It was late in the evening and I was getting ready for bed when I saw his car come into the driveway. I noticed that he didn't come into the house. When I went outside, I found him in the driveway. We rushed him to the hospital, but he did not regain consciousness. He died from a cerebral aneurysm. We never knew he was affected by it."

Peter is eloquent in his description of twin loss: "At the time of death, a twin does not realize how important the relationship was. The living twin is immediately thrust into a world that is unfamiliar, the world of being an only person. This is a world that we have a hard time understanding because we have spent so much time literally and metaphysically with that other person.

"I have run the gamut of emotions, from unbelievable sadness, to a rage that I had never before experienced," Peter shared. "The emotions come and go quite suddenly. You may be having a good day when all of a sudden something reminds you of your loss and instantly, you start sobbing. The best piece of advice that I ever got was from a friend of mine, Jeff Crull. He said, 'Just let it hit you.' When I stopped trying to prevent myself from feeling bad and actually let it 'hit me,' I felt much better."

Larry Lynch, forty-five, has a similar story. "I lost Garry in a single vehicle accident one and a half blocks from my house. He had just left to avoid an argument I was having with my wife over him. She had given me an ultimatum — him or me — so I was helping her pack to leave."

Larry continued, "To me the loss a mother feels for her child is about one percent of the loss I feel for my twin. A mother loses a part of herself with the child; I lost a half of me. When Garry died, I lost the one and only person who provided me with unconditional support.

"I lost Garry twenty years ago. I still struggle on the anniversary of his death, but take great comfort in watching my son, Josh, grow up. He exhibits more and more of Garry's personality each day. That is a great comfort to me now."

No matter how much good advice, grief counseling, or attempts at self-healing, most twins say the pain never truly goes away. Sometimes it's even harder when the connection was so strong that both twins felt physical trauma at the time of death. Paul Heiden is 47 years old. He lost his twin, Pete, less than a year ago. He knew what was happening even though he and his brother were two hundred miles apart.

"When Pete had his heart attack, I knew something was happening. I had extreme hot flashes and my whole body shook. I started to sob uncontrollably while standing in my kitchen. I had had a strange feeling that whole afternoon—like just before a storm. I was restless and sensed that something was terribly wrong.

"Just four hours earlier, I had taken Pete to the airport after a four-day visit with him. It was a cherished visit. I was the last one to see him, hug him, and talk with him before he went into a two-week coma and died. I don't think it was a coincidence that we were together," Paul said.

"I have always felt like a half of a whole. I hated it when I was younger but came to appreciate it more as Pete and I got older. The novelty of being different was fun after we had established separate identities and lives. I was always asked, 'What's it like to be twin?' I would always answer, 'What's it like NOT being a twin?' I was not being smart; it was my reality. Today I often feel like a huge part of me is missing—like I am no longer complete. It is a very strange experience and impossible to describe.

"What do I cherish the most? I cherish the wonderful experience of having someone who was so much like me. Someone with whom history need not be discussed. We had the exact childhood experiences, so we could always refer to them without explanation. We experienced a sameness and connectivity that allowed for a 'shorthand' communication. I will always cherish our ability to laugh to tears about things—usually to the dismay of others who didn't have a clue as to what we were laughing about. I miss Pete all the time."

For Brenda Haugen, thirty-eight, twin brother Brad had truly been her best friend. She grew up with a disability, but he had made her feel special. "He made me feel like I didn't have a disability and that I belonged somewhere. He treated me just like a person. He did not discard me. He knew my limits. The loss was devastating for me because I felt like a part of me was ripped out and gone for good."

Like many others, Brenda experienced a lot of emotions. She even considered suicide. "I was unable to eat or sleep for long periods of time," Brenda said. "There were times when I felt really depressed, very hurt and lonely. I also felt misunderstood about my loss. The one thing that helped me the most was going to the Twinless Twins International Convention. There I met someone very special to me. She had lost her twin the same way I lost mine—in an accidental drowning. It happened the same month and in the same way. Today we share the same fears. She has helped me feel more comfortable about myself."

Having a loved one snatched from your life, especially someone with whom you have shared a womb and created history is traumatic no matter what the circumstances. For twins, it's often hard to figure out why the sibling was chosen and not you. The questions become even more complex and unanswerable when twins take their own lives. For the surviving twin, it's almost impossible to comprehend why your twin might choose to end his or her life when the bond is so strong.

"Verna and I were close for fifty-one years," said Joann Schimpf, now fifty-two. "We grew up in a suburb of Chicago and then moved to Boca Raton, Florida. We graduated together in the first graduating class of Boca Raton High School. She was named the first football queen. I was so proud of her.

"We looked alike growing up, but I always thought she had the more bubbly personality. I think I was the more serious twin. We were like Mutt and Jeff. Our teacher called us 'the double trouble twins.' We did everything together.

"There is nothing like a twin connection. Being born together means you are alike, think alike, and have a connection no other sibling could possibly feel. We had very strong ESP.

"Verna suffered from bi-polar disorder (euphoria/depression)," Joann explained. "She had gone through a difficult divorce and many setbacks. She suffered from insomnia and was tired all of the time. It was very sad because the doctors said they couldn't do much for her situation. When she took her own life, she was at a stage where no one could help her—not even me. I was constantly trying to lift her spirits and keep her in an upbeat mood, but it was to no avail. It was a really difficult and sad time.

"I have been through emotions of extreme sadness,

full of tears, and the feeling that half of me is no longer there. I know and have pretty well accepted the fact that, with the grace of God, she will be with me in spirit for the remainder of my life. I thank God that I have a supportive family to help me get through losing her."

Sudden death rears its ugly head in many ways—through unforeseeable accidents, suicide, and murder. Death by the hands of another human being is perhaps the most unforgivable. The surviving twin gets cheated out of a lifetime of companionship and memories.

David Jones, fifty-six, is one such twin who lost his brother, Dennis, to a senseless act of homicide. "I lost my twin on December 5, 1970. He was murdered as he entered his own home. Two guys were robbing his house and they killed him to keep him from talking. It later came out in the trial that he knew them both. We were twenty-six years old at the time. Even now, when it's thirty years later, it still feels like yesterday."

David and Dennis (nicknamed Naner) were the second set of twins out of nine children. They were given up at birth and were adopted by wonderful parents at the age of three.

"My twin and I had our own language, which we developed while we were being passed around to different families," David said. "We were very close to each other. Even though we had separate beds we'd always end up sleeping together when we were little. Wherever you found one of us, you'd find the other. We did most things together—played sports, double dated, shared clothes, shared classes. We even signed up for the Marines together on the 'Buddy Plan.'

"We could talk to each other without ever saying a word out loud. This really amazed our friends. What I cherish the most was always having someone to confide in and to seek advice from. I loved being able to call at any hour and talk about anything. We always knew each other's secrets were protected. I have two younger brothers and I love them very much, but I can't talk to them like I used to talk to my twin. To this day, I miss him very much.

"When people ask me how I feel, I tell them that I still feel an empty space inside me," David continued. "I feel incomplete. I feel alone. I miss my best buddy, my soul mate, my second mind. The emotions I go through each day are the same: hate, sadness, anger, love, emptiness, solitude. Some days are worse than others. And this goes on each and every day since his death."

Incomplete

The men and women who have lost their twins as adults are the lucky ones, say people who lost their twins in the womb or at birth. They had the good fortune to get to know their sibling, at least for a while. The pain is still as great, but they have memories to cherish, photographs to examine, and fond stories to tell with love and affection.

There are many twins though, who lost these partners in life at a very early age. One might think that there would be no pain—that there would be no memory of the other and life would evolve as if they were singletons. That simply is not the case.

Linda N. Rutherford lost her twin in the womb, prior to birth. Medical professionals call it "intrauterine demise" and the "vanishing twin syndrome." Generally one twin may not be as healthy as the other and for whatever reason that twin is absorbed into the mother's body.

"Having lost my twin before birth and not learning of it until the age of forty makes my experiences somewhat different from those who had earthly time with their twin. For many years, the loss was more like a vague vapor coming in waves. On some intuitive level, I knew there was something 'more,' yet I was never able to articulate what I was feeling. I think I resolved that my feelings of incompleteness were simply how life was and attributed them to the external circumstances," Linda said.

"Most of my life I resisted my life because there were no explanations that could actually define my experiences until now. I think I give myself greater permission to feel all my feelings now, and I am not so resistant. Today I am much better knowing that many of my character attributes come from my experience as a twin. I believe the neurological pathways still exist. I am now working to resolve the sadness, incompleteness, uneasiness, and unbalance that was a big part of my life."

Part of Linda's awakening came from her discovery of a book about Elvis Presley. *The Inner Elvis* was written in 1996 about the great entertainer's life and how the loss of his twin brother, Jesse, at birth, became something that would haunt him and drive his entire life.[15] Psychologist Peter Whitmer writes: "Elvis Presley had a twin brother, perfectly formed, seemingly a mirror image to him, but stillborn. He had been born, in fact, as one of a pair. Elvis's twin's death at birth was a tragedy that triggered a process that made his dead sibling the bedrock, the singular driving force in his life. Understanding the complexities that shape a twinless twin is the key that unlocks the mystery of Presley's motivations, his behavior, and his special power. Jesse Garon Presley continued to live, a restless spirit who eventually haunted all of Presley's relationships."

While the "haunting" of twinless twin Elvis Presley may sound a little extreme, the effects of losing a twin at birth are indeed real. Mary Anne's life has been rich but also riddled from time to time with sadness.

"I lost my twin sister, Anne Marie, at birth. My mother was thirty-five years old, pregnant for the first time, and two weeks overdue. I weighed seven and a half pounds and Anne Marie, who was the bigger twin at eight pounds, was in the breech position. After Mother labored twenty-six hours, the doctor decided to attempt forceps deliveries. He delivered me first and as he struggled to bring Anne Marie into the world, she was strangled by her own umbilical cord. Many years later, he admitted to us that his inexperience and inability to handle such a complicated delivery had cost my twin her life.

"I must have always sensed my loss because my mother later told me that I seemed to talk to another person when I was a baby and a toddler. I once heard her say she wondered if she had done something wrong to cause my twin's death. I often wondered the same about myself."

Mary Anne's adolescence was filled with "trying for two." She tried twice as hard to please her parents. "I was an excellent student, well mannered, and obedient, and yet I never felt I was doing enough," Mary Anne said. "I believe I was trying to be perfect so that my mother would be satisfied with her 'one.' I even felt at times that I was competing with my twin who I imagined would have been smarter, prettier, and not as fat."

Mary Anne continued, "I once heard an interview with Elvis Presley who was talking about his twin Jesse. He said he felt so empty that nothing could fill the space. Finally, someone spoke my feelings. Most interesting was the similarity of his loss to my own and the sadness of his mother. I believe Elvis achieved all he did to give her happiness, and that he tried twice as hard to please her. This seems to be a common thread among early-loss twins as they try to replace their twin by their own double efforts."

Mary Anne has been happily married for thirty-six years and has three sons, three daughters-in-law, and four grandchildren. Yet she says there are still times when she feels the overwhelming loneliness she experienced as a child. "There is always a place inside that misses someone who never shared the light of day with me. There is a need for love still unmet. I am blessed to have such a wonderful family and yet I still feel incomplete at times. That is the legacy of twin loss. We will always have a connection; even death cannot break it."

Teena Wood, forty-eight, also feels the never-ending pain of twin loss even though she never knew her twin. Teena explained, "I lost my twin at birth. She lived just three hours. We shared a womb together for seven months. How close can you get? I did not realize until I had completed a lot of therapy in my mid thirties and early forties how impacted I was by her loss. It affected my ability to have close relationships and to feel that I even deserved happiness in the world. I felt responsible for her death and had survivor's guilt. Finally, in my forties, I grieved her loss for the first time. It was very poignant for me and also bittersweet. But I felt like I'd been set free. I felt as though I'd just gotten out of my own prison and I'd been the one with the key all the time.

"Today I feel more at peace," Teena continued. "Though I still have times when I feel a deep loneliness and a wish to have my twin close by me as an adult. I know we would be close today and share much of our lives together."

Debbie Farbrother, forty-three, lost her twin, Donald, three days after birth. She found out later in life when her mother gave her the laminated death notice from the newspaper. That clipping and a vase that sat on her twin's grave are the only two things she has that physically validate that she is a twin.

"As a child, I always felt different from my other siblings," Debbie said. "This is a natural feeling, I have discovered, for many who have experienced an early loss of a twin. It's like I needed to fill a void that I just couldn't explain.

"At the age of sixteen, I couldn't stand myself. I even wrote a poem about dying, which showed that I was in such a lost state of mind. I couldn't explain or talk about missing my twin. Why? No one believed I could miss someone that I had never met because he hadn't lived for more than three days. That's how it was. No talking about it. It was as if 'it never was.'

"Early-loss twins always feel that empty feeling," Debbie added. "The loss and mourning continue throughout our lives. It's not quite like other twinless twins who have been able to share their lives to some degree. We feel cheated out of a totally different life. Our lives would have been so much richer had we been able to share our living days with our twins. People don't realize that. And yes, we are jealous—not simply envious—of those who did share their lives with their twins. That's the honest truth."

A Child's Loss

It's impossible for me to imagine a child losing a sibling, let alone his or her twin. I shudder to even think about it as it might relate to my own family. The pain surrounding the "what if" scenario is far too painful to even consider for a split second. But twins do lose twins in childhood. Karl Ellis lost his twin, Kathy, at eight years of age. He is now thirty-four and still feels the loss—all the time.

"Kathy and I weren't allowed to be close," Karl explained. "She suffered brain damage when we were babies. She had been dropped and hit her head. She never learned to walk or talk and was in the hospital a lot. She died because of complications from a massive heart attack. Still I feel like my heart was sliced open and left to bleed without the prospect of healing.

"Some days I mercifully forget my twinship," Karl continued. "It's not for long. It's always there. Other days I look to the sky and scream, 'Why? What did I do? Why do you punish me without end?' Twin loss is more than just losing a loved one. It's losing a part of one's self that can never be replaced. As twinless twins, we are forever cursed to seek something we know we will never find in anyone but our twin."

Together in Spirit

"Margaret and I used to go to the beach when we were feeling down," said Mary Hartung Wetter, forty-four. "When she died, she wished to be cremated and her ashes put into the water. Now, when I go down to the water and talk to her, I feel at peace. It's like she's there and she's listening to me."

The spiritual connection between twins can be very strong whether they are together, separated by distance, or separated by death. Many believe they share each other's souls, and you have to wonder, in the case of identical twins, when the egg splits and each twin gets half of everything, if that includes the soul and spirit.

One of the most profound twin connections I have heard about belonged to Jill Mertinke, fifty-one, and her sister, Judy. "When Judy died I lived in Wisconsin and she lived in Colorado. The morning she died, she was having some minor female surgery. She went in at about 9:30 A.M. and was to be out by 11:30 A.M. Around 10:30 A.M. I had a spiritual type of experience within me telling me that she was dying. I brushed it off as a bad thought. At about 1:00 P.M., I got a call from her husband saying that she had died in surgery. Her heart had stopped."

Most of the blending of spirits is associated with death. Joyce Durren still feels connected to her twin, Joanne. "I know Joanne and I are still connected. And I know what she looks like—her little, bright, golden soul dances around me when I need it the most. I feel her energy. I have had dreams about her but not many. I did have one very significant dream, or vision, soon after my son died that also gives me confidence about her. I was sleeping and thought I was dreaming but she came and told me he was okay. I have never felt that kind of happiness in my whole life. So when I feel Joanne, I know she is also close by."

Dreams and visions can play a key role in helping twinless twins get past some of their pain. Michele Turner recalls one particular dream: "About a month after Michon was killed, I was at my mother's house. I was asleep. I could smell my sister's breath and her perfume, and I could hear her. She came to me and said she was okay and that her daughter, Tori, who had also been killed in the plane crash, was also okay. That never happened again to me with anybody. At first, the whole thing scared me, but then I took great comfort in her words."

Michele continued, "I think of her all the time and I can feel her with me. She is still in my dreams. There are times that I pray to her for strength and I pray that she can see her kids. There is one thing about being a twin, when something like this happens, I'm not anxious to die, but I am not afraid of it either."

Lori Neiwart, thrity-eight, still feels a spiritual connection with her twin, Mike, who was killed in a car accident. "I have dreams in which he is telling me something important, but I haven't figured out what that is. I no longer feel his heartbeat as I did throughout his life, but I feel his spirit. When I have been at my saddest I have felt him touch me to comfort me. I feel like he is watching over me."

Many twinless twins believe that they have a special someone watching over them. Teena Wood is no exception. "I still feel very connected to my twin," she said. "I know she is my guardian angel, watching over me and guiding me. I have often felt her beside me or near me. The experience is nothing in particular, just a sense or feeling. While I was writing, I felt as though she were writing through me. Once I went to an astrologer/psychic and she told me that had my twin lived she would have been a writer."

After Thelma Ellis lost her beloved twin, Velma, to a lengthy and serious illness, she had a very specific spiritual experience that gave her great comfort. She had been in a lot of pain after Velma's death. Thelma remembers, "I had a dream after she died. In this dream, we were both on an Army base. She was dressed in Army fatigues and she had a clipboard in her hand. She came around the barracks walking very strong with her head held up and her shoulders back. She said, 'Heavy (my nickname from birth), I have finished my assignment. You have to finish yours.' I felt so different after that dream. I thanked the Lord because she did finish her assignment. And when she passed away she was so weak and ill, but in this dream, she was strong and beautiful.

"After that I was able to get out of bed and get back to my life," Thelma added. "I am applying what she said. I have a purpose and an assignment here, and I have to finish it up. That's what makes me go on. To this day, I still have dreams about her, but they aren't as vivid as that one."

After talking to many twinless twins, I am convinced there is a spiritual bond that remains in place and endures through the years. Gail Rubinfeld believes this, too. "One day after Miri died, my husband and I were talking about all the difficulties of her illness. There was a crash in the closet in our bedroom. All our pets were accounted for, so even my husband was nervous. Was there an animal in there? No, instead we found my twin's diary on the floor. It was turned to her morning pages. We also found the book *The Artist's Way* on the floor. ["Morning pages," an exercise from *The Artist's Way*, are written each day as a way of freeing up one's creativity.] Miri was an artist and gave me the book to read as a way to encourage me to paint. The books never fell before or since. And I felt like she was telling us she was there.

"I feel very connected to Miri every time I look in the mirror. She is there. I see her face looking back at me. It's a comfort and a constant reminder that she is gone now. It is a blessing and a curse. Most people get to forget sometimes after a close relative dies. But not a twin. I did learn this summer how lucky I was that I had Miri for forty-six years, while others lost their twins as youngsters or at birth. I learned not to be jealous seeing other twins. I am saddened that one of them will eventually be a twinless twin too."

Tom Carlock, who lost his twin, Tim, believes his connection is still strong. Tom said, "I have experienced visits from Tim since he has died. He promised me when I was taking care of him that he would visit if he could. Tim died at fifteen minutes past midnight on August 6, 1998. That morning, around six o'clock, I awoke and sat up in bed. My cat of eight years,

Anastasia, was staring at a fixed point beside my bed. I knew Tim was there; I could feel his energy touch my left shoulder. I heard a crow caw outside my window and then he was gone.

"Since then, when I feel despair and feel like giving up or joy when I remember something special we shared, I'll spy a single crow waiting for me. Tim knew the symbolism of the crow and he knew that it would always get my attention.

"My most recent spiritual experience happened when I returned to Jamaica—the place I had fled to a week after Tim died," Tom continued. "This trip was, of course, different, but it did bring up memories. I was sitting in the living room when I turned to my right, and I saw Tim sitting on the edge of the couch. He had a rich glow around him and a smile on his face. He looked happy and not in pain. The radio I was listening to went dead for about thirty minutes while I talked to Tim. And even though I only actually saw him for an instant, I knew he was there. I spoke to him about the loss I was still experiencing and how badly I missed him. At the end of the conversation, the radio came on right at the beginning of a song that Tim and I used to sing together in the year before he died.

"I do still feel very connected to Tim and know that I always will. I feel that he is with me, in my heart.

When I experience bad days, I think about that and the sadness dissipates. The anniversaries of his death, our birthday, and holidays are extremely hard, but I get through each of them knowing that one day we'll be together again."

The Impetus to Growth

Twin loss can be devastating, as these stories have told. But in at least one case, the loss forced a twin to blossom into her own person and gain the self-confidence she might never have known. Jill Mertinke, fifty-one, was an identical twin to Judy.

"I believe that studies have shown that many times one twin is more dominant than the other," said Jill. "Such was the case with Judy and me. Judy didn't seem to need me as much as I needed her for my identity. Therefore, when she died in surgery twenty-two years ago, the impact was somewhat overwhelming.

"I married soon after she died, so instead of being Judy's twin I was now Harvey's wife. When we divorced sixteen years later, I once again found myself without an identity. In fact, taking on a new identity without fully dealing with my twin loss came back to me after my divorce. I actually picked up the phone and tried calling Judy, and she had been dead for almost twenty years.

"It hit me like a huge bang on my head," Jill continued. "Who was I? Was I still a twin? Was I going to attach myself to another person's identity? To make a long story short, I began college at the age of forty-one. I received my bachelor's degree in psychology when I was forty-five. I completed my master's degree in counseling psychology at fifty and have now passed the Licensed Professional Counselor exam.

"Today, I am emotionally, spiritually, and mentally very happy. I miss Judy tremendously, especially at milestone times for me such as my graduation from college. I missed having her beside me when our brother and then our father died. And I missed her the day I got my first job as a counselor in my new profession.

"What I want people to understand most about twin loss is that although a twin is gone, there will always be a soul connection," Jill said. "I want them to understand that there is an emptiness inside, but I also want them to know that a twin should strive to heal. They can and should evolve into a separateness while maintaining closeness. It can be done. I am a living example."

Loss of a loved one, no matter what the circumstances, is hard on anyone, but for twins, it seems even harder still. A look in the mirror, a birthday spent alone, or a stranger's faux pas over a mistaken identity can trigger new depths of loss and grieving for a twin. For the majority of twinless twins, their loss rarely diminishes and as a result, lasts a lifetime.

CHAPTER NINE

Resources

There are many books available today on the subject of twins, covering everything from what to expect when you're pregnant with multiples and how to raise twins, to famous twins and explicit scientific twin research. While *Twin Stories* focuses on the fascinating life experiences of twins themselves, I also want it to serve as a resource for anyone who might come into contact with twins in their lifetime—families, friends, educators, counselors, and clergy, to name a few. On that note, I am passing along what I consider to be valuable information and insight.

Support for Parents of Twins

When my husband and I found out we were having twins, we were elated. We also had a bit of parental confidence under our belts because our first son was nearly two. We had survived midnight feedings, sleep deprivation, and assorted other challenges that come with any new baby. To give us further strength and confidence, I joined the Brevard County, Florida, chapter of The National Organization of Mothers of Twins Clubs, Inc. NOMOTC was founded in 1960 for the purpose of promoting the special aspects of child development that relate specifically to multiple birth children.

It was such a wonderful group—not only of mothers but also of families. They welcomed me with open arms even though my babies were not due for a few months. I enjoyed listening to the stories of their twin adventures. They seemed quite bonded to the other women in the organization and shared tips, swapped clothes, and even offered in-home assistance to new mothers who were trying to cope with the non-stop activities of newborns.

It wasn't until after my twins were born that I truly came to appreciate the women in the group. After Sam and Max were born, I remember looking around the meeting room in amazement. These women were champions. They had raised two babies at one time and lived to tell about it. They were my inspiration during the hard times, and my respect for them was immense. Some of the women had given birth to two sets of twins! One young woman, about twenty-three years old, was a single mom, raising her babies by herself and going to college. She had little support, yet she was happy, healthy, and successful.

The National Organization of Mothers of Twins Club is a network of some 450 local clubs representing over 22,500 individual parents of multiples—twins, triplets, and quadruplets. Its goal is to improve public awareness of the needs of multiple birth children by fostering development of local support groups; enhancing the quality of educational materials available to parents, educators, and others; and by cooperating with and participating in research projects which involve twins and/or their families. It is a nonprofit corporation funded by dues, donations, and grants.

Rearing twins is hard. I had the help of a very supportive and hard-working husband and my parents. Still, I needed the support of other women who had gone through the experience. They gave me moral support and advice, which I still use to this day. I think that anyone who is preparing for twins or who is in any stage of rearing these precious people should investigate the Mother of Twins Club.

Twinsburg—
A Sanctuary for Twins

The 2000 Twins Days Festival in Twinsburg, Ohio, was such a phenomenal event for me. From the moment I approached the registration area on the first night to the moment I got on my plane to head back to California, I carried a feeling that something special had happened to me. Who could have imagined such a magical place? And I'm not even a twin.

For the past twenty-five years, the Twins Days Festival has been honoring twins, triplets, and others of multiple birth from around the world. When I walked in, the place felt like one giant high school reunion, only the people came in pairs of all ages, backgrounds, ethnicities, and sexes. Many twin sets did not know each other, yet they greeted one another like long-lost friends. The camaraderie was so thick and infectious that I wished I were a twin. I actually felt like an outsider because I didn't have a mirror image with me. I dearly wanted my twins to experience the moment and celebrate their twinness with all of the others.

I certainly wasn't alone in my feelings. Linda Houk, forty-two, twin to Laura, recalls her first reaction. "I went home and told everyone I couldn't believe that we didn't feel out of place. We don't have to hear 'Are you sisters or twins?' We can dress alike and feel good about it. It feels right. It was the best experience."

Upon their first visit, Renee Richardson and Rhonda Kulpinski, thirty-four, needed a little more encouragement. They had spent many years and a lot of energy trying to erase the twin stigma. "Our first year here, we met a lot of twins who talked about how close they were," said Renee. "A lot of them still lived together and worked at the same place and shared the same vehicle. We thought we were on the freak side of it because we're not like that at all. We are really individuals." Rhonda added, "We really love Twinsburg now. We have realized there's a place for us and it's not out of the ordinary for us to celebrate our twinness anymore."

The Twinsburg Twins Days Festival is almost like a safe haven for twins. It's a time and place where they can rejoice in the fact that they are twins. They wear their twinness like a badge of honor, displaying it in the annual parade, the look-alike contests, and the annual rendezvous with friends made in years past. I met one group of three sets of twins who have made the pancake breakfast a ritual for the past six years. They don't communicate with each other during the other 362 days of the year, but they know that come the appointed time, all six of them will meet, share stories and scrapbooks, and celebrate a friendship that was created and endures because of their commonality.

Jackie Gagnon and Jeannine St. Hilaire, forty-four, talk about their first time at Twinsburg. "The first year we came with our families," said Jackie, "our families recognized that this was a special place for us and a special time to be together. Since then we have come alone. They fully understand it. And we appreciate this weekend. We are so thankful we get to come. This is our once a year time together."

Jeannine added, "We are the majority here. There is so much going on here that everyone should know about it. I think it is a wonderful thing. The more attention this festival gets the better."

Unless you have been to Twinsburg, it's hard to understand what a gift the festival is to twins. The entire town is transformed into a mecca of doubles. The twins are extraordinarily friendly and stop in the middle of the street just to greet other twins. Most pairs are dressed alike regardless of whether they are identicals or fraternals. The festival is colorful and upbeat. It feels like Christmas or the Fourth of July. And the twins feel safe. They are not a spectacle. They are not stared at. They're just like everybody else.

Tara Behnke and Christine Rizzo, thirty, sum it up. "Some people just can't understand it; they think coming to Twinsburg is a freaky thing to do," said Christine. "They can't understand that we look forward to this event all year long because we love these people." Tara added, "Everyone here can relate to one another. It's nice for a change. When you get here, everyone understands how you feel because they've shared a lot of the same experiences as you—including finger pointing. Even when we talk to other twins, often one of us can relate to one twin and the other to the other twin. We love coming here."

Twinless—But Not Alone

For twinless twins, there is also a place where they can feel safe and get the support they need. Raymond W. Brandt, Ph.D., Ed.D., an identical twin whose twin, Robert, was killed at the age of twenty, founded the organization, Twinless Twins Support Group International. Its mission is to support twins (and all multiples) who suffer from the loss of companionship of their twin through death, estrangement, or in-utero loss.

"Grief lasts a lifetime," Dr. Brandt said. "Since the bond does not end until both twins die, that bond remains a constant reminder of their twinship, which again stirs pain, frustrations, and sometimes happy memories. I am a self-accomplished person with many credentials and honors, yet it frustrates me that I cannot rise above my pain. I founded Twinless Twins out of desperation in 1983.

"I have been asked many times on twenty-seven national and international talk shows what it feels like to be twinless and each time I struggle, for our semantics are geared to single-birth expressions. No words have ever been coined that allow me to explain the fine details of the pain I feel daily for Robert's loss. Just imagine cutting yourself into one half and you begin to get a hint of the pain and incompleteness we feel after losing our twin."

Under Dr. Brandt's leadership, the organization has grown to more than two thousand members, despite the fact that he does most of the membership recruitment, support, and publicity on his own time and at his own cost. The twinless twins gather annually for a conference where they share their stories and encourage each other. Between conferences they have a very active network of twinless twins who telephone, write, and e-mail each other. Many have found this communion with other twinless twins an immense help in their lives. Dr. Brandt believes twinless twins can understand each other's feelings like nobody else can.

"For me, the Twinless Twins organization has been a blessing," said Mary Hartung Wetter. "My beloved daughter, Jennifer, discovered the group and introduced me to it in my time of need. When you're really hurting, you let the organization know and it sends out a message saying a twin is in crisis. It really helps to get the support from other twins who have the same feelings and have experienced this tremendous loss. I, myself, have helped a few twins in crisis."

Debbie Farbrother says the group has helped her as well: "My mother came with me to a Twinless Twin conference in 1996. She found out for the first time just how much the loss of my twin was on my mind. It was the greatest thing that could have happened to me—having my mom know just how I felt. No other person in my family has experienced that with me and now at least one person knows after all of these years! I am so grateful and thankful to Dr. Brandt for this major event in my life."

Twinless Twins maintains a database and e-mail roster of all of its members. It also publishes a quarterly newsletter, *Twinless Twins,* in which twinless twins can contribute letters, articles, or poetry. It also helps medical and holistic professionals who are treating and counseling surviving twins.

"As founder and director of Twinless Twins, I have an honorable cause to continue lifting other twinless twins from the deep mire of their loss," said Dr. Brandt. "I have never met a twinless twin who said that he or she is totally over their twin's demise."

Twin Wisdom

No one knows better than twins themselves just what a gift they have been given. Who better to offer parting words of wisdom to other twins than the people in this book?

"There are a few things I would say to all twins," said Brenda Haugen, twin to Brad. "I would say that you need to be there for each other, support each other in good times and in bad, and resolve any conflicts you might have so that you can enjoy your bond."

"If you have a twin, you are very fortunate," said Joyce Durren, twin to Joanne. "You are fortunate because you have a bond that can never be broken. Just communicate in the way that is special to you and your twin, and cherish your relationship—even the rough parts. Appreciate the many things you have in common and respect the things in which you don't agree."

David Jones, twin to Dennis, has more encouragement. "Be each other's best friend, pal, buddy, soul mate, and 'there-when-you-need-me' twin. No matter what happens during your growing years, always be there for your twin. Always protect each other. Share everything you can with each other. And enjoy your twinship because it is very special. One thing, with my twin, is that we never came right out and said, 'I love you' because we both knew we did not have to speak the words."

"I hope twins who still have each other will learn to cherish this gift while it exists," said Karl Ellis, twin to Kathy. "You share a bond that singletons will never know. And we share a loss when our twin is gone that singletons will never know as well."

As most twins will tell you, they *are* special. Most are blessed with a lifelong partner who provides unconditional love at its purest. They share history— some of it good and some of it wrought with challenges. They grow and learn and love together. For many, being a twin means much more than just a lifetime of deep connection and spirituality. Twins recognize their twinness as a great and wondrous gift—one that they will cherish throughout their lifetimes and beyond. It's a gift that we, as singletons, will never know, but can still acknowledge and celebrate in friendship and in love.

Notes

1. Nancy L. Segal, *Entwined Lives: Twins and What They Tell Us about Human Behavior* (New York: Plume, 1999), 6.

2. Peter Whitmer, *The Inner Elvis* (New York: Hyperion, 1996) 8.

3 George H. Napheys, *The Physical Life of Woman: Advice to the Maiden, Wife and Mother* (Philadelphia: H. C. Watts & Co., 1884), 160-161.

4. Ron Hutcheson, "Bush's Twin Girls Avoid Publicity," *San Jose Mercury News,* 25 May, 2000, A-8.

5. "The 50 Most Beautiful People in the World 1998: Seeing Double When Celeb Twins Meet Their Match, It's Deja-you All Over Again," *People,* 11 May 1998.

6. *Entertainment Tonight Online,* Spotlight Stories, www.etonline.com.

7. Nancy L. Segal, *Entwined Lives,* 3.

8. E.M. Bryan, *The Nature and Nurture of Twins* (London: Bailliere Tindall, 1983).

9. The Twins Days 2000 Festival program, Twinsburg, Ohio, 49.

10. Patricia Malmstrom, "Good Twin, Bad Twin," *Twins Magazine,* July/August 2000.

11. Ashton Applewhite, William R. Evans, III, and Andrew Frothingham, *And I Quote,* (New York: St. Martin's Press,1992), 70.

12. Nancy L. Segal, *Entwined Lives,* 22.

13. Applewhite et al, *And I Quote,* 57.

14. A. S. Berman, "Twins Double-Click with This Web Site," *USA Today,* 14 September 2000, 3D.

15. Whitmer, *Inner Elvis,* 9.

Appendix

The Center for Study of Multiple Birth (CSMB)

The Center for Study of Multiple Birth is recognized internationally as a unique resource for research and information about the causes, effects, and problems of multifetal pregnancy. Peer professionals, multiples and their families, and the print and electronic media look to CSMB as the authoritative source of information in its field.

CSMB
333 East Superior Street, Suite 464
Chicago, IL 60611
(312) 908-7532
(312) 908-8500 Fax
http://www.multiplebirth.com

The National Organization of Mothers of Twins Clubs, Inc. (NOMOTC)

The National Organization of Mothers of Twins Club is a network of 450 local clubs representing over 22,500 individual parents of multiples (twins, triplets and quadruplets).

NOMOTC
P. O. Box 438
Thompson Station, TN 37179-0438
(877) 540-2200
http://www.nomotc.org

Twins Days Association

The Twins Day Association is the organization that holds the annual Twins Days Festival. Held every August since 1976, this three-day event takes place in Twinsburg, Ohio.

Twins Days Association
P. O. Box 29
Twinsburg, OH 44087
(330) 425-3652
http://www.twinsdays.org

The Twins Foundation

The Twins Foundation is an international membership organization and primary research information center on twins and other multiples. It serves twins, their families, the media, medical and social scientists, and the general public through its publications, its National Twin Registry, and its multimedia resource center.

The Twins Foundation
P.O. Box 6043
Providence, RI 02940-6043
(401) 729-1000
http://www.twinsfoundation.com

Twinless Twins International

Twinless Twins International was created to support of twins (and all multiples) who suffer from the loss of companionship of their twin through death, estrangement, or in-utero loss.

9311 Poplar Creek Place
Leo, IN 46765 -9352
(219) 627-5414
Twinworld1@aol.com (e-mail)
http://www.fwi.com/twinless

Twinstories.com

Twinstories.com is a further extension of this book where twins, families and friends of twins, and twin experts can share their stories by posting them on the Web. Twins can gain from the personal experiences of others and rejoice in their twinness.

Twinstories.com
P.O. Box 769
Twain Harte, CA 95383
(209) 586-5887
http://www.twinstories.com

Twinslist.org

This list is intended for discussion of *all* aspects of twins. Though a lot of the day-to-day discussion revolves around survival strategies and equipment purchases for new parents of twins, triplets or more, discussion of other topics is very welcome. Visit http://www.twinlist.org.

About the Author

Susan Y. Kohl, APR, is a former broadcast journalist and public relations executive. She is the founder of Sierra Communications, a virtual public relations agency with operations in California and Texas (www.sierra-comm.com). She has won numerous awards for her public relations and marketing efforts, and is an accredited member of the Public Relations Society of America. Prior to her career in PR, she worked as a radio and television news journalist for CBS Radio, WCPX-TV in Orlando, Florida and KCOY-TV in Santa Maria, California. She also served as host for PM Magazine, Montana.

Twin Stories is Susan's second book. She is also the creator of twinstories.com, a creative outlet for twins, friends, and families of twins, and twin experts to share their personal stories. The website is found at www.twinstories.com. Susan also authored the book *Getting Attention: Leading-Edge Lessons for Publicity and Marketing* (Butterworth-Heinemann) in 2000. She holds a Bachelor of Arts degree in Communications from California State University, Chico.

Susan is the mother of identical twin boys. She lives in the Californian Sierras with her husband, Doug, and sons Frank, Sam, and Max. She can be reached through e-mail at skohl@sierracomm.com or through the www.twinstories.com website.

About the Press

Wildcat Canyon Press publishes books that embrace such subjects as friendship, spirituality, women's issues, and home and family, all with a focus on self-help and personal growth. Great care is taken to create books that inspire reflection and improve the quality of our lives. Our books invite sharing and are frequently given as gifts.

For a catalog of publications please write:
Wildcat Canyon Press
2716 Ninth Street
Berkeley, California 94710
Phone: (510) 848-3600
Fax: (510) 848-1326
Email: info@wildcatcanyon.com
Visit our website at www.wildcatcanyon.com

More Wildcat Canyon Titles

In the Dressing Room with Brenda: A Fun and Practical Guide to Buying Smart and Looking Great
Personal Shopping advice from Brenda Kinsel.
Brenda Kinsel
$16.95 ISBN 1-885171-51-X

40 over 40: 40 Things Every Woman Over 40 Needs to Know About Getting Dressed
An image consultant shows women over forty how to love what they wear and wear what they love.
Brenda Kinsel
$16.95 ISBN 1-885171-42-0

girlfriends Get Together: Food, Frolic and Fun Times!
The ultimate party planner from the best-selling authors of the girlfriends series
Carmen Renee Berry, Tamara Traeder, and Janet Hazen
$19.95 ISBN 1-885171-53-6

Life Is Not Work; Work Is Not Life: Simple Reminders for Finding Balance in a 24-7 World
A little book of wisdom for everyone who wants to find a balance between work and the rest of life.
Robert K. Johnston and J. Walker Smith
$13.95 ISBN 1-885171-54-4

MOVING FROM FEAR TO COURAGE: TRANSCENDENT MOMENTS
OF CHANGE IN THE LIVES OF WOMEN
A fascinating and inspiring look at brief moments of
insight, which allow women to live beyond their fears
and change their lives forever.
Cheryl Fischer and Heather Waite
$13.95 ISBN 1-885171-50-1

THE MOTHER'S COMPANION: A COMFORTING GUIDE TO THE
EARLY YEARS OF MOTHERHOOD
Here's a book as delightful to hold (almost) as a newborn
baby, and friend as true as any for every new mother.
Tracy Marsh with Sharon Hauptberger and Lisa Braver
Moss
$20.00 ISBN 1-885171-59-5

SOARING SOLO: ON THE JOYS (YES, JOYS!) OF BEING A SINGLE
MOTHER
Companionship, comfort, and reassurance for women
with the most difficult–but rewarding–job of all: being a
single mother
Wendy Keller
$13.95 ISBN 1-885171-60-9

LIFE AFTER BABY: FROM PROFESSIONAL WOMAN TO
BEGINNER PARENT
An emotional compass for career women navigating
the unfamiliar seas of parenthood.
Wynn McClenahan Burkett
$14.95 ISBN 1-885171-44-7

STEPMOTHERS & STEPDAUGHTERS: RELATIONSHIPS OF
CHANCE, FRIENDSHIPS FOR A LIFETIME
True stories and commentary that look at the relation-
ship between stepmother and stepdaughter as strong,
loving, and a life-long union.
Karen L. Annarino
$14.95 ISBN 1-885171-46-3

BOUNTIFUL WOMEN: LARGE WOMEN'S SECRETS FOR LIVING
THE LIFE THEY DESIRE
The definitive book for women who believe that
"bountiful" is a way of being in this world, not a par-
ticular size.
Bonnie Bernell
$14.95 ISBN 1-885171-47-1

AND WHAT DO YOU DO? WHEN WOMEN CHOOSE TO
STAY HOME
At last, a book for the 7.72 million women who don't
work outside the home—by choice!
Loretta Kaufman and Mary Quigley
$14.95 ISBN 1-885171-40-4

GUESS WHO'S COMING TO DINNER: CELEBRATING CROSS-
CULTURAL, INTERFAITH, AND INTERRACIAL RELATIONSHIPS
True-life tales of the deep bonds that diversity makes.
Brenda Lane Richardson
$13.95 ISBN 1-885171-41-2

CALLING TEXAS HOME: A LIVELY LOOK AT WHAT IT MEANS
TO BE A TEXAN
Bursting with fascinating trivia, first-person accounts
of frontier days, curiosities, and legends of the people
of Texas.
Wells Teague
$14.95 ISBN 1-885171-38-4

CALLING CALIFORNIA HOME: A LIVELY LOOK AT WHAT IT
MEANS TO BE A CALIFORNIAN
A cornucopia of facts and trivia about Californians and
the California Spirit.
Heather Waite
$14.95 ISBN 1-885171-37-4

CALLING THE MIDWEST HOME: A LIVELY LOOK AT THE
ORIGINS, ATTITUDES, QUIRKS, AND CURIOSITIES OF
AMERICA'S HEARTLANDERS
A loving look at the people who call the Midwest
home–whether they live there or not.
Carolyn Lieberg
$14.95 ISBN 1-885171-12-9

AUNTIES: OUR OLDER, COOLER, WISER FRIENDS
An affectionate tribute to the unique and wonderful
women we call "Auntie."
Tamara Traeder and Julienne Bennett
$12.95 ISBN 1-885171-22-6

LITTLE SISTERS: THE LAST BUT NOT THE LEAST
A feisty look at the trials and tribulations, joys and
advantages of
being a little sister.
Carolyn Lieberg
$13.95 ISBN 1-885171-24-2

girlfriends: INVISIBLE BONDS, ENDURING TIES
Filled with true stories of ordinary women and
extraordinary friendships, girlfriends has become a
gift of love among women everywhere.
Carmen Renee Berry and Tamara Traeder
$12.95 ISBN 1-885171-08-0

girlfriends FOR LIFE: FRIENDSHIPS WORTH KEEPING
FOREVER
This follow-up to the best-selling girlfriends is an all-
new collection of stories and anecdotes about the
amazing bonds of women's friendships.
Carmen Renee Berry and Tamara Traeder
$13.95 ISBN 1-885171-32-3

A girlfriends GIFT: REFLECTIONS ON THE EXTRAORDINARY
BONDS OF FRIENDSHIP
A lively collection of hundreds of quotations from the
girlfriends books series.
Carmen Renee Berry and Tamara Traeder
$15.95 ISBN 1-885171-43-9